# How to Design and Deliver Quality Service Training

**The Kogan Page Practical Trainer Series**


**Series Editor: Roger Buckley**

# How to Design and Deliver Quality Service Training

**TONY NEWBY**

KOGAN PAGE
Published in association with the
Institute of Training and Development

First published in 1992

Apart from any fair dealing for the purposes of research or private study, or criticism or review, as permitted under the Copyright, Designs and Patents Act, 1988, this publication may only be reproduced, stored or transmitted, in any form or by any means, with the prior permission in writing of the publishers, or in the case of reprographic reproduction in accordance with the terms of licences issued by the Copyright Licensing Agency. Enquiries concerning reproduction outside those terms should be sent to the publishers at the undermentioned address:

Kogan Page Limited
120 Pentonville Road
London N1 9JN

© Tony Newby, 1992

**British Library Cataloguing in Publication Data**

A CIP record of this book is available from the British Library.

ISBN 0 7494 0737 9

Typeset by Koinonia Ltd, Bury
Printed and bound in Great Britain by Biddles Ltd., Guildford and King's Lynn

# Contents

# Series Editor's Foreword

Organizations get things done when people do their jobs effectively. To make this happen they need to be well trained. A number of people are likely to be involved in this training: identifying the needs of the organization and of the individual, selecting or designing appropriate training to meet those needs, delivering it and assessing how effective it was. It is not only 'professional' or full-time trainers who are involved in this process; personnel managers, line managers, supervisors and job holders are all likely to have a part to play.

This series has been written for all those who get involved with training in some way or another, whether they are senior personnel managers trying to link the goals of the organization with training needs or job holders who have been given responsibility for training newcomers. Therefore, the series is essentially a practical one which focuses on specific aspects of the training function. This is not to say that the theoretical underpinnings of the practical aspects of training are unimportant. Anyone seriously interested in training is strongly encouraged to look beyond 'what to do' and 'how to do it' and to delve into the areas of why things are done in a particular way.

The authors have been selected because they have considerable practical experience. All have shared, at some time, the same difficulties, frustrations and satisfactions of being involved in training and are now in a position to share with others some helpful and practical guidelines.

In this book Tony Newby tackles an area that has increased rapidly in prominence: quality service. In the experience of many of us this has meant short-term campaigns encouraging staff to smile, use customers' names, wish them a nice day and so on. Such campaigns frequently begin with earnest commitment and exhortation from 'the top' and, after the initial impetus, lose momentum and are reduced to a few out-of-date posters and tired slogans.

Quality service means much more than this. It has now become a feature of competition between commercial organizations and a measure of efficiency of non-commercial organizations and of those who serve the needs of staff within their own organization. There are few of us who could claim that we do not have 'customers' in some sense of the word. These customers have expectations of us and quality service involves setting those standards of quality which customers should expect and against which an organization's performance can be measured.

To get it right, there is a need for systematically planned training to ensure that it is implemented properly and a need for the total and continuous commitment of everyone in the organization.

This book provides sound guidelines for trainers, line managers and supervisors who are involved in the introduction, implementation or maintenance of quality service.

ROGER BUCKLEY

# Introduction

Quality of service training is concerned with improving the service to those customers without whom the organization would not exist, by means of improvements in the ways in which the organization operates internally. It is about solving customer service problems, both externally in the market place and internally within the enterprise. It is also about responding to the continually-evolving upward curve of customer expectations.

The book offers a guide to the design and delivery of organization-wide programmes which have the aim of measurably changing the quality of the service delivered to customers. The book is not concerned with technical issues of manufacturing quality. The quality approach can be used with equal value in both commercial and non-commercial contexts, with any size of organization.

## Is This Book for You?

The primary audience for whom this is written is the professional trainer but the book is also intended to be a helpful working document for all 'informal trainers': line managers, supervisors, sales and marketing managers, and those technical and professional specialists in disciplines outside personnel and training.

There are few managers who do not have some element of training responsibility in their job. Even when managers do not directly deliver training, they often play a key role in the related decision-making, in ensuring that what has been learned through training subsequently gets used in the workplace, and in addressing the question of value for money, or cost-effectiveness, of training. Such informal trainers may find *Cost Effective Training – A Manager's Guide*[1] (also published in the Practical Trainer Series) a helpful foundation.

It is also important that managers at all levels play an active role in the process of creating a quality service culture. Of course, no training or organizational change task should be undertaken without management support to ensure its utilization in the workplace, but quality as an issue demands even more commitment and active participation.

This book is intended to assist trainers to design quality of service programmes that make a measurable difference and to assist managers and others to contribute to and reinforce such programmes by showing where their contribution is necessary and how it can be made most beneficial.

This is designed to be a practical how-to-do-it book. It spells out in clear, step-by-step fashion how a fully integrated quality service training programme can be put together by the in-house trainer using internal and/or external resources. The book is written for people at the sharp end of organizations, whether private or public sector, and avoids academic debate. It is intended to be a self-contained guide and, apart from a very few suggestions, does not send you chasing off to find other books or obscure articles.

## The Focus of the Book

This is a guide to the design and delivery of organization-wide programmes which have the simply-stated, though in reality complex, aim of changing the measurable quality of the services delivered to customers. The book is not concerned with technical issues of manufacturing quality, although some of the processes that are described may well have appropriate applications in that context.

The overall strategy and the techniques that I describe can be used with equal value in both commercial and non-commercial contexts. The framework can be directly applied, or easily adapted, to any kind (and size) of company or non-profit operation. The content of the tasks and the exercises by which people will learn to create a quality culture is based on the real working environment of each specific organization. For convenience, I shall refer to the recipients of any organization's services as the 'customer'. However, other words may apply in other contexts, eg:

| | | |
|---|---|---|
| client | patient | passenger |
| tenant | borrower | purchaser |
| visitor | punter | sponsor |
| applicant | patron | guest |
| shopper | consumer | member of the public |

I do not feel that it is necessary to replace well-established descriptive words that are specific to a particular sector, or are commonly used in the population at large, with the all-embracing term 'customer'. There is a very real risk that this can be seen by employees and recipients of the service alike as merely a cynical and superficial re-labelling, used to avoid real and necessary changes in the quality of customer service delivery. However, it is also important that any term used to describe recipients of a service does not acquire derogatory or patronizing undertones: in such instances, a move to using the more neutral 'customer' may well be an improvement.

---

PRACTICAL TIP

• Don't let the organization kid itself that a problem re-labelled is a problem solved.

---

## How to Use this Book

Each chapter begins with an outline summary. As well as the explanatory text, often broken down into precise instructions on how to carry out particular tasks, you will find various exercises, checklists and the like which are labelled 'Activities'. These are provided to help you to relate the book content to your own organizational situation. There are also a number of sections headed 'Practical Tips' which offer ideas which will, I hope, live up to the heading.

Chapter 1 explains how improvements in service quality call for much greater depth than the traditional 'smile' campaign and demand integrated measures that will be implemented by everyone from chief executive to new entrant. The limitations of 'quality awareness' as a training goal are made clear. The necessity of management commitment is stressed, both in terms of personal involvement and of resourcing. The concept of quality standards as benchmarks of training results and as reinforcement of good corporate and departmental practices is introduced. The internal customer chain and the role of quality action teams are outlined.

Chapter 2 discusses what is meant by 'quality' in a customer service context. The methods for diagnostic research to underpin quality training are examined. Management's role in quality service training is described, including the use of corporate mission statements. The process of management briefing cascades is outlined and guidance provided on designing an initial 'wake-up' training event.

Chapter 3 describes the organizational support structure required for quality service training. Advice is provided on recruiting and training a pool of 'temporary trainers'; on the creation of a quality council to oversee the project; and on the formation of problem-solving action teams. Reward and recognition options are examined together with the development and monitoring of quality performance standards.

In Chapter 4, the concept of the internal customer service chain is introduced. This forms an essential base for delivering quality service to external customers. The role of an internal customer working party to steer this element of the programme is described. There is guidance on the design and delivery of an internal customer training event, including the training of temporary trainers, the development of materials for trainers and participants, and guidance on the use of video and case studies.

Chapter 5 describes how to make quality action teams a central part of the quality service training programme: the structuring of the action teams and their activities; the initial information cascade to all employees; the selection and training of team leaders, mentors and team members; the development of working materials for the teams; and the choice of pilot projects. The cycle of meetings for each team is described and the place of rewards and recognition considered.

The final chapter considers the design of a training workshop to enhance quality service skills. It describes the formation of a quality service skills working party and the development of support materials for trainers and participants with extensive examples. The development of temporary trainers is considered, with specific guidance on techniques for interpersonal skills training. Lastly, issues in the validation of quality service training are described and specimen measurement instruments illustrated.

NOTES

1. Tony Newby, *Cost-Effective Training – A Manager's Guide*, Kogan Page, 1992

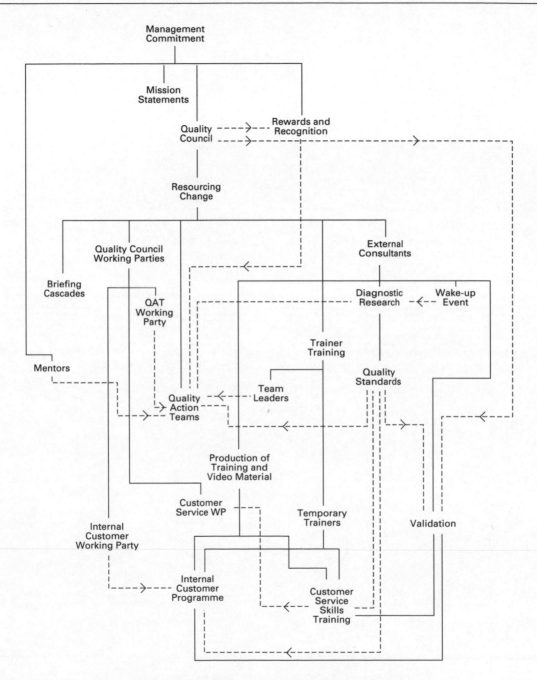

*Flow Chart Overview of Quality Service Training*

# 1 The Elements of Quality Action

▷ SUMMARY ◁

Improvements in service quality call for much greater depth than the traditional 'smile' campaign and demand integrated measures that will be implemented by everyone from chief executive to new entrant.

The idea of an integrated quality of service programme, suitable for both commercial and non-commercial organizations, is introduced. The limitations of 'quality awareness' are indicated. The necessity of management commitment is stressed, both in terms of personal involvement and of resourcing. The concept of quality standards, as benchmarks of training results and as reinforcement of good corporate and departmental practices is introduced. The internal customer chain and the role of quality action teams are outlined.

## Quality Programmes – An Overview Of The Main Elements

A quality of service programme is different in ambition and intensity from a single-focus training topic such as 'interviewing' or 'interpersonal skills'. First, it involves everybody, without exception. Second, to succeed, it must consist of a number of separate – though linked – measures that include management processes, administrative procedures, the reward system, setting standards of performance, measuring quality of work output, and skills training in the narrower sense. This range of measures is outlined in this chapter and then developed in depth in subsequent chapters.

---

## PRACTICAL TIP

- Never lose sight of the fact that improving service quality is a complex task, which demands concurrent improvements in a number of different directions and must involve all levels of the organization.

## Quality Awareness

There may sometimes be an initial, preparatory step that an organization needs to go through, during which employees at all levels are encouraged to think about quality of service both as a concept in general ('what does "quality" mean?') and as an issue of particular concern in their own enterprise ('why quality matters here'). However, such awareness activities are no more than a curtain-raiser; they should never be confused with the more substantial activities that must follow if lasting change is to be achieved.

Indeed, the first question to ask about *any* programme with the word 'awareness' in its title is: 'Will it be a waste of money and effort?' – and the presumption should always be 'Yes, until proven otherwise'. Usually, the weasel-word 'awareness' indicates training in the 'nice to know' rather than 'need to know' category; typically, 'awareness' events are what you end up with when neither trainer nor management client knows clearly what they want to be done differently at work.

Unfortunately, ambitions for change are not always matched by the appropriate means – sometimes the more grandiose the change goals, the more superficial the methods adopted. However, you cannot expect major shifts in long-established patterns of behaviour as a result of brief, under-researched, and unreinforced events, however flashy the presentation. Beware, too, of 'badge engineering' which typically involves putting your corporate logo on the front cover of an otherwise standard package of material. 'Tailored' programmes can only justify that description if they are based on substantial in-house analysis of training needs and contain a substantial proportion of material that is specific to the commissioning organization. External suppliers may collude with a buyer's unrealistic expectations, for the very human reason that there is a lot of money to be made. 'Snake oil training' and 'blessing the crowds with a hosepipe' are two popular judgements from those on the receiving end.

You cannot have cost-effective training without accurate diagnosis of needs, which means going out into the workplace to discover just what it is that people need to learn in order to become more effective in their jobs. This is as true of 'quality' programmes as of any other subject of training. Diagnosis starts from such questions as 'What are people doing (or not doing) that needs to be changed?', or, 'What would you, the manager, like to *see* people doing differently after they have been trained?' The emphasis must be on the *observable* behaviour that needs to be changed, or introduced.

This emphasis on observable work behaviour is central to making 'quality' something that is practised, not just talked about. It sidesteps the problems created when training needs are stated in terms of 'awareness' or 'attitudes'. We should recognize that personality change is difficult to achieve, takes a long time, and lies within the remit of therapists rather than trainers.

---

### PRACTICAL TIPS

- Beware of the hype and glitz that surround a lot of customer service or quality of service training: go for the substance of change first and sort out the presentational packaging later.
- Start with a diagnostic approach: what kinds of behaviour and practice in the workplace need to change?

---

## Management Commitment

What will managers at all levels in the organization say and do to help make service quality a reality? Their contribution is partially a matter of giving visible support and partially a matter of providing adequate re- sources for quality initiatives. Managers have a key role in setting the quality agenda, spreading the quality message, and reinforcing good service quality practices that training has introduced; these contributions are explored in detail in Chapter 2.

At a policy level, there need to be clear corporate standards of quality and behaviour, linked to consistent marketing messages (what the or- ganization promises, it must deliver). Administrative procedures must not sabotage the best efforts of employees to be responsive to customers. Management style should reward good customer service behaviour by employees and not allow short-term panics to undermine long-term credibility.

Conversely, if you are asked to pursue major changes on a shoestring budget, that tells everybody precisely how little your efforts are valued. If lip-service to training is paid by senior managers, with the implicit mes- sage of 'Do as I say, not as I do', then middle and junior managers will usually follow that example and the training input will sink without trace.

---

PRACTICAL TIPS

- Involve managers in the programme right from the start.
- Encourage managers at *all* levels in the organization to lead by example.
- Ensure that the reward system does not discourage managers from playing a constructive role in service quality initiatives.
- Equip managers with the skills they need in order to contribute to service quality activities.

---

## Quality Standards

Standards play two distinct roles in an organization-wide quality of service training programme. First, there need to be yardsticks for the improvements to service quality that you are seeking. The process of setting goals and benchmarks is itself a valuable part of the whole quality of service programme and methods will be described in Chapter 3. The benefits of such benchmarks are that:

- training is focused: learners know what is expected of them;
- the outcomes of training can be measured;[1]
- you know how near to your goals you are (and organizational sponsors can get feedback on progress – and on obstacles);
- achievements can be appropriately recognized and rewarded.

Second, standards of performance themselves form a component of the total programme. Minimum standards of performance can be set for key service tasks, both those that apply across the whole enterprise and those that apply to a single department or even a single section. Developing and implementing such standards is a very effective element in learning about quality; it also links into other aspects of the overall training, notably those concerning the role of managers, and those involving quality action teams.

---

PRACTICAL TIP

- Ensure that all training, procedural and management elements of your quality of service programme are linked to explicit, measurable standards of performance.

---

## Internal Customers

A core element of service quality programmes is to ensure that all members of the organization know who their own internal, as well as external, customers are. Everybody in an organization either directly serves customers or helps colleagues (internal customers) who contribute to a chain of customer service that eventually reaches an external customer.

The internal customer chain of service can start to break down when 'them and us' barriers develop, eg:

- between the sections in a process chain (where different people handle different stages of a document, for instance);
- between head office and branches;
- between sales and marketing;
- between marketing and manufacturing;
- where one part of an internal chain deals with an external customer in such a way as to cause problems for other parts of the chain.

A significant part of quality service training is therefore focused upon activities which help employees to identify their own role as an internal customer, its relationship with other parts of the chain, and its impact upon the external customer. Chapter 4 offers detailed guidance.

---

### PRACTICAL TIP

- There is usually at least one department or section which will try to opt out 'because they do not deal with customers'; if that were true, there would be no need to continue employing them ... and your service quality programme would already be showing a positive cost-benefit justification! But, of course, one result of your training programme should be that they change their perception of their role *vis-à-vis* customers (and change their work behaviours in line with this).

---

## Quality Action Teams

One of the most under-utilized resources is the grass-roots job knowledge of the 'average' employee. Their experiences and frustrations – and their energy to improve matters if they are given the opportunity – are what make quality action teams a powerful problem-solving element in the quality process.

Quality action teams consist of small groups of (usually) lower-level employees who meet regularly and work within a structured framework to identify and resolve problems that affect their ability to deliver the best possible quality of service. Chapter 5 describes in detail how to set up, train, and run such groups.

---

PRACTICAL TIP

- Quality improvements mostly come about as a result of numerous small improvements, rather than a few major changes, and the people who are best positioned to make such improvements are mostly located at the lower end of the organizational hierarchy.

---

ACTIVITY

Before investing more of your time reading how to design and deliver quality service training, it may be as well to make a preliminary assessment of the need for such an initiative – and of the likely response from your organization. The following checklist offers some questions that may help provoke discussion between yourself, your peers, and your clients.

1. What evidence do you have (systematic or anecdotal) that quality of service to customers needs attention?

2. What is the trend (a) relative to how things used to be in your organization; (b) relative to the trend amongst your competitors?

3. List the five worst instances of poor quality of service that you've heard about in the last year. Try to make (or obtain from line or sales managers) an informed guess about what each of those instances has cost (a) directly; (b) in secondary damage (eg, to reputation and hence to subsequent business).

4. Is your 'gut feel' that those five worst instances were untypical – or were they the tip of the iceberg? In either case, what is it all costing (in money, morale, damage to clients, credibility, etc.)?

5. Does it start to look as though there is enough of a problem, and a big enough potential benefit to the organization, to make it worth carrying out a thorough diagnostic process?

6. Who will welcome such a quality of service initiative? What benefits do you think they anticipate?

7. Who will be neutral? What will win them over?

8. Who will oppose it? What objections do you think they will raise? How can you make best use of such objections, if they really are raised?

9. You are looking at potentially major changes and substantial resourcing. Who will approve the project? What will influence the decision?

10. Do you really want this project? Is it an exciting challenge for you, or a source of anxiety?

## Chapter Review

Making change happen is partly a matter of getting your goals in clear view and partly a matter of such political skills as persuasion, influence and the ability to build alliances. The trainer who is embarking upon quality service training will be working as a catalyst of change, not simply a provider of conventional courses, and this requires a number of additional skills:

- entry skills that enable you to get access to the people who have the information you need or whom you need to influence;
- developing relationships – establishing rapport with people, understanding their points of view and needs;
- diagnostic abilities that enable you to analyse the situation and develop solutions that work in both a technical and a political sense, getting commitments to action and generating resources.

To achieve improvements in service quality calls for much greater depth than the traditional 'smile' campaign. It also demands that a range of integrated measures are adopted, that will be implemented by everyone from the chief executive to the newest trainee. Nobody can stand outside the service quality process.

This chapter has provided an introduction to the idea of an integrated quality of service programme, suitable for both commercial and non-commercial organizations. The limitations of an 'awareness' focus have been spelled out. The necessity of management commitment has been stressed, both in terms of personal involvement and of resourcing. The importance of quality standards has been indicated, both as a benchmark for achievement within training and as a reinforcement of 'quality' in corporate and departmental activities. The concept of the internal customer chain has been introduced as has the role of quality action teams which harness the problem-solving energies of the average employee.

**NOTES**

1. Tony Newby, *Validating Your Training,* Kogan Page, 1992

# 2 Creating the Climate

▷                 SUMMARY                 ◁

This chapter discusses what is meant by 'quality' in a customer service context; it then reviews what is different about good customer service. Quality awareness is distinguished from quality action. The importance of diagnostic research as a foundation for training is emphasized and the main directions for, and methods of, such research are examined. Management's role in quality service training is described, including the use of corporate mission statements. The process of management briefing cascades is outlined and guidance provided on designing an initial 'wake-up' training event.

## Introduction: Quality And Customer Service

Quality of service training is concerned with improving the service to those customers without whom the organization would not exist, by means of improvement in the ways in which the organization operates internally. It is about solving customer service problems, both externally in the market place and internally within the enterprise.

Customers have expectations which are often set by other industries and not just those that are similar to the sector in which you are operating. These expectations are continually evolving and growing more demanding, so that standards of service quality always need to be on an upward curve.

Furthermore, the 'How' is frequently as important as the 'What': competing goods and services often do not differ greatly from each other, so the manner in which they are supplied can become more important than the product or service itself, both at the point of sale and in follow-up after-sales provision. Adequate service often registers as poor by comparison with other organizations. If your customer service is merely 'adequate' then it is probably invisible to customers – only excellent service gets noticed.

The core elements of 'quality service' can be stated quite simply; the complexity comes from the measures that are essential to move the organization from where it is now to where it wants to be (or needs to be, for commercial survival). In summary, quality of service to the customer is about:

- meeting and exceeding customer expectations;
- avoiding complaints happening, by getting things right first time;
- zero defects in products and services;
- continuous active searching for ways to improve the quality of the work for which each employee is responsible.

This definition of 'quality of service' is not set in stone. It must adapt over time, as people use 'quality' ideas and adjust and extend them to fit their own particular and changing circumstances. Quality action teams, line managers, formal reviews of performance standards, skills training all play a part in putting real meaning and substance into the concept of quality – meanings that will inevitably evolve over time.

## What Is Different About Good Customer Service?

Quality service is about the quality of what you deliver to customers and the quality of how you deliver it. It is not a smile campaign! Good service is based upon the basic truth that no business or institution survives in the long term by taking a short-term view of its customers – if they don't come back, if their friends, relations and acquaintances do not come back, there is no future. Most dissatisfied customers don't tell you. They tell their friends, with embellishments. Will your customers 'write it off to experience' and go elsewhere next time? Or, are you creating an organizational culture where people will want to come back?

Customer service is a mixture of knowledge and skills which are learned, not innate. Quality service reflects a thorough knowledge of:

- the products or services you supply;
- the external customers for those products and services;
- the systems and procedures of your organization;
- the network of internal customers with whom you work.

Quality service reflects competence in the essential customer service skills:

- getting things right the first time;
- listening to customers and responding constructively;
- handling complaints in a positive way;
- being assertive when under pressure;
- communicating clearly;
- making it easier for colleagues to help customers.

Everybody in an organization has to work at service quality to get it right, but most of the improvements needed to achieve excellence require a lot of very small changes in the way people work day-to-day, rather than a few very large-scale projects that probably will never happen.

Quality customer service has three main benefits:

- survival of the organization;
- greater job security for employees;
- positive self-image and job satisfaction for the individual.

---

PRACTICAL TIP

Make these three points the foundation and manifesto for your service quality programme:

1. *Everybody* has to work at service quality.
2. Most improvements require a lot of very small changes, rather than a few big projects.
3. Quality service skills are learned, not in-born.

---

## Quality Awareness And Quality Action

I have described in Chapter 1 why the focus of the quality training programme needs to be *observable workplace behaviours* rather than 'attitudes' or 'awareness'. I have also suggested that there may need to be an initial, preparatory step that has to be gone through, during which employees start to think about what 'quality of service' might mean for the ways in which they work. This concerns both the general question of 'What does "quality" mean?' and the rationale for action – 'Why quality matters here'.

Once your quality programme gets under way, there will inevitably be those who either deliberately or through lack of understanding criticize the training on spurious grounds. It is, then, useful to spell out what the quality service training is *not*. It is not...

- a company suggestion scheme;
- a substitute for managers managing;
- workers' control;
- an opportunity for whingeing;
- a smile campaign in which everyone goes around saying 'Have a nice day'.

Nor is such a programme a quick fix: a properly-designed and carried-through quality service programme, in a medium-sized organization (say 3–5,000 people), is likely to need around eighteen months to two years to progress through the various stages, so that new ways of working become embedded in the corporate culture.

## Diagnostic Research

Accurate diagnosis of service quality change needs means not only going out into the workplace but also into the customer environment in order to discover what is required. The emphasis must be on the *observable behaviours* that need to be changed, or introduced.

The areas for enquiry are likely to include at least the following:

- corporate strategy on quality;
- management practices;
- administrative procedures;
- customer service skills. Do all staff know how to deliver high quality customer service, face-to-face or on the telephone? Do they need help to be better able to handle complaints, enquiries , sales opportunities, or internal-customer teamwork?
- work standards. Are there defined standards of performance against which employees are measured? Are such standards linked to quality and service concepts – or to throughput of paperwork?
- rewards and recognition opportunities.

Training needs to fall into two broad categories: someone is not doing a job as well as they are capable of doing, due to some shortfall in their knowledge or their skills (a remedial need) to do things better; or, someone needs to acquire additional knowledge or skills in order to perform new or amended work tasks in the near future (an anticipatory or developmental need). The essence of a training need, then, is a gap between what exists and what is needed for optimum performance. The extra factor that needs to be considered when the subject is customer service is what are the needs and expectations of the internal and the external customer and are these expectations being met?

The diagnostic research phase has two aspects: the market environment, and the customer interface. The first can be addressed by a method such as SWOT analysis (Strengths, Weaknesses, Opportunities, Threats) which seeks data on the organization's present and future standing in the marketplace. These data may be indicative of current training needs, or may highlight developmental needs for the future.

The second aspect, the customer interface, is concerned directly with the service quality issues that will feed into the training programme content. This diagnostic process looks at such question as:

- who are the customers for the organization's outputs? (Note that 'customers' are not necessarily just the end-consumers of a product or service; there may be intermediate customers such as wholesalers, purchasing agents, advisers, and the like);
- what aspects of service quality are salient for each group or type of customer?
- how well are these salient aspects of customer service being met at present?
- what potential improvements can be identified?

Diagnosis investigates such performance and behavioural questions as:

- What are people doing that they ought not to do?
- What are people not doing that they should?
- What are people doing adequately that they need to do well?
- How are these various activities perceived by customers?

This is a market-led approach to training that mirrors the principles of marketing applied to products and services. Training needs analysis is the equivalent of market research applied to consumer products. One benefit of the marketing-led approach in training is that all those consulted during the research phase can feel ownership of the proposed solution to their problems. It becomes more realistic for managers to think of training as an investment in their staff rather than a tax on their resources. Following on from this, they are more likely to play a reinforcing role pre- and post-training. Trainers themselves benefit from better quality of information on which to base their training designs.

A further, major benefit from systematic diagnostic work is that post-training evaluation of cost-effectiveness is made easier: properly-defined learning objectives incorporate the criteria by which the trainer or manager can assess the extent to which that objective has been met. It is a much more laborious task to add evaluation measures retrospectively to an existing training design.

It is outside the remit of this book to discuss diagnostic techniques in detail: these are covered more comprehensively in a companion volume.[1] However, some applications of diagnostic techniques are suggested below:

- *Performance appraisal:* useful to identify service quality training needs at an individual level, provided the manager knows what he or she is looking for.
- *Critical incident diary:* a self-report technique for identifying quality training issues within the workplace; useful where such issues may crop up at irregular and unpredictable intervals.
- *Behaviour observation:* a third-party technique for identifying service quality training issues within the workplace; especially useful where skill deficiencies need to be analysed and their occurrence can be predicted.
- *Job analysis:* a non-empirical method, by which quality aspects of a job role may be identified by a subject expert; useful where you are planning training for a newly-created job.
- *Analysis of performance data:* when appropriate indicators are used (see Activity, following) can indicate problem areas requiring closer investigation, using observational techniques.
- *Interview:* particularly valuable when gathering data from both external and internal customers, because the technique allows detailed exploration of problems encountered and the feelings these have engendered.
- *Questionnaire:* typically of limited value, partly because questions are rarely very searching (as well as often being badly-drafted); partly because response rates are usually low (often because customer opinion surveys are seen as exercises in self-justification by the organization, rather than as genuine attempts at improvement).
- *Opinion survey:* employed with staff or customers; if the results show negative staff attitudes or customer dissatisfaction on service quality issues, may be useful as a 'frightener' to persuade management into action; staff opinions may give results at variance with empirical data of bad customer service practices, widespread complaints, and so on; and must be supplemented by behavioural diagnostics in order that appropriate training can be developed.

---

### PRACTICAL TIP

- Diagnostic research is the single most important part of the entire quality service programme – it underpins all parts of it and must be the last element that you cut back on if resources are tight.

| ACTIVITY | | | |
|---|---|---|---|
| **Inadequate service quality which may respond to training** | | | |
| *Examples of service quality problems* | *Does it happen here?* | *Best guess at £ cost* | *Best guess at £ gain by training* |
| **Customers seen as a nuisance** | | | |
| **Faults found before delivery** | | | |
| **Faults found after delivery** | | | |
| **Delays in response to customer queries** | | | |
| **Loss of market share** | | | |
| **Accidents to customers** | | | |
| **Delivery delays** | | | |
| **Stock problems** | | | |
| **Contract deadlines missed** | | | |
| **Promises not kept** | | | |
| **Poor internal communications upwards and/or downwards** | | | |
| **Blaming of other departments** | | | |
| **Poor interpersonal skills in customer contacts** | | | |
| **Absenteeism/bad timekeeping** | | | |
| **Procedures that serve the organization, not customers** | | | |
| **Excessive staff turnover** | | | |
| **Shortage of promotable staff** | | | |
| **Friction between sections or departments** | | | |
| **Belief that customer service only matters for people who directly contact external customers** | | | |
| **Inadequate knowledge of products/ procedures/organization when speaking with customers** | | | |
| **Absence of consistent measures of work performance** | | | |
| *Think of your own examples* | | | |

## Management Role In Quality Service Training

Good customer service reflects the whole corporate culture. It is based upon not just the knowledge and skills of the individual but also upon the way that the organization as a whole, from top management downwards, pulls in the same direction and presents a clear, positive message to customers. This reflects:

- policies – clear corporate standards of quality and behaviour, linked to consistent marketing messages (what the organization promises, it must deliver!);
- administrative procedures – that make quality service possible and do not sabotage the efforts of employees to be responsive to customers;
- management style – that actively rewards good customer service behaviour by employees and does not allow short-term fire-fighting to undermine long-term credibility.

There are two useful inputs that the trainer can draw on, in order to kickstart management involvement in the service quality process: the corporate mission statement, and the diagnostic data.

### Mission Statements

The preliminary question is, of course, 'Does a mission statement exist?' Has the organization developed a clear policy statement concerning its major goals? How widely has this been communicated? Above all, does it make the slightest difference to how people do their jobs?

A mission statement serves several functions – it is a banner to rally around, a guide for action, a symbol of corporate identity. However, all mission statements risk being treated cynically, as statements of the 'do as I say, not as I do' variety, or else as 'motherhood truths' of such vague generality that no-one can disagree with them, but neither is anyone influenced to work differently. Management exhortation realizes at best only a fraction of the motivational potential that a good mission statement can generate in employees.

The factor that really makes a mission statement 'take off' is a sense of *ownership* on the part of the people who are asked to act in line with it. It is therefore particularly important that any mission statement is made the foundation for an action programme to ensure that the messages of the statement are translated into measurable good work practices. Such a programme takes the core messages of the mission statement and turns them into corporate and localized performance standards. The mission statement ceases to be a statement of intention and becomes 'the way we do things here'.

This can be achieved through a series of short workshops that cascade down from the centre to local level. Workshops are needed for every level of management, for professional staff, and for clerical, technical and unskilled employees. The workshops enable individual employees to define clearly for themselves what the mission statement means in day-to-day operational terms, as it affects each person's own job.

## Management Commitment

Managers' contribution to quality training is partially a matter of active involvement in the processes of change and training (most directly as regards policy and procedural issues, quality action teams, performance standards, and the mission statement; indirectly through support for customer skills training and action on internal customer service). It is also a task for management to provide adequate resources for quality initiatives.

In the early stages of quality service training-managers have a key role in setting the quality agenda (based on the diagnostic research) and in spreading the quality message through an information cascade. Later, they have the essential task of reinforcing the good practices that training has introduced.

---

PRACTICAL TIP

- Ensure that managers who play an active and constructive role in service quality initiatives are recognized and rewarded.
- Ensure that all managers are fully briefed about the necessity of the quality service initiatives before the programme rolls out to other employees; work from the top downwards.
- Resolve (at as senior a level as it takes) any resistances towards the proposed programme from individual managers: which does the organization need more...?

---

## How Managers Can Make the Difference

To get the quality of customer service your organization needs, managers must lead by example.[2] Furthermore, they should resist the trap created when an over-cautious policy of 'pilot projects' is instituted: the reality is that any individual employee alone is very unlikely to achieve major changes in the quality of customer service in your organization – management needs to build up a critical mass of people who are pulling in the same direction. Even when a pilot extends to a whole department, there are usually so many issues that spill over departmental boundaries that the guinea-pig group is more likely to end up frustrated and hostile than keen advocates of the quality measures.

The positive role that managers can play in quality service training can be summarized as follows:

- helping trainers to diagnose learning needs;
- ensuring that the right people are matched to the right training;
- briefing subordinates so that they know what benefits they can expect from the training;
- de-briefing returning trainees to check out what they have learned and agreeing a timetable for putting it into practice;
- allowing subordinates to do things differently and tolerating occasional mistakes during the learning stages;
- providing constructive feedback on subordinates' performance when they try out new knowledge and skills – and reinforcing effective ways of working;
- acting as a role model, guiding mentor and coach;
- evaluating the cost-effectiveness of the investment the organization has made in quality service training.

## The Management Briefing Cascade

The rationale for a briefing cascade is that it harnesses the numbers, the status and the need for involvement of senior, middle and junior managers in order to communicate information, generate commitment, and progress various elements of the quality programme.

The concept of a management briefing cascade is very simple. Each level of management briefs its subordinate level. This process saves on the expense of external presenters (except, usually, at the very start of the cascade where the top team should be briefed by the training department or the external consultants). The cascade process gives the whole quality programme the organizational credibility and authority that it needs if it is to succeed.

There are two training requirements linked to the cascade: one is to provide key-point notes for the managers who will conduct briefing sessions; the other is to ensure that they have the presentation skills necessary for effective delivery.

The briefing cascade is not a one-off process, but one that is repeated at successive stages of the quality service programme. Sometimes, the same information will flow down through all levels of management; on other occasions, there may be sensitive information which needs to be restricted to certain people. The most likely purposes for management briefing cascades are the following:

- to convey the findings from the initial diagnostic research; introduce the overall structure of the quality service training programme (eg, performance standards, internal customers, quality action teams, customer service skills); and create the management framework for the whole programme (eg, quality council);
- to develop the organizational mission statement into performance behaviours and standards;
- to approve corporate and departmental standards of performance and associated recognition and reward elements;
- to brief managers on the detailed operation of quality action teams and to recruit team mentors;
- to brief managers on the detailed content of skills training events.

## Creating And Running A 'Wake-Up' Event

I have commented in Chapter 1 on the limited value of 'awareness' training. Nevertheless, there may be a need for some kind of initial activity to catch the attention of managers and employees, simply to start them thinking about service quality issues. A short, high-profile training event, fronted by top management, can be useful. It may also be an opportunity to bring together employees who do not usually meet, although this may raise issues of the balance of logistical costs and organizational benefits if people need to be transported considerable distances.

This is not a problem-solving event. It should be structured to raise issues, without solving them. It should inspire with a vision of the future that leaves participants with the urge to get up and do something about those issues. The overall message must be that this is an organization-wide initiative, with total support from the top, and everyone will take part in it.

The data from diagnostic research can be presented in very broad-brush summary, highlighting the main implications for the organization (and people's jobs). A summary of 'service quality' topics can be presented together with the outline of the training activities that will, over a period of around 12 to 24 months, address those issues. Aim small:

big themes sound impressive but are likely to paralyse initiative ('That problem is too big for me to deal with'). It is worth emphasizing that changes will come about from hundreds or thousands of small improvements of the kind that your audience can themselves make, rather than from a few great leaps forward.

The event should be up-beat in tone, short and to the point. It should send participants out of the door feeling excited by the potential each individual has to make a contribution that will be recognized and valued.

## Chapter Review

Quality of service training is concerned with improving the service to external customers by improving the ways in which the organization operates internally. If the quality of customer service is perceived to be merely 'adequate' then it is probably invisible – it is only excellent (or atrocious) service that gets noticed.

In summary, quality of service to the customer is about meeting and exceeding customer expectations; avoiding complaints by getting things right first time; and about actively searching for ways to improve the quality of the work for which each employee is responsible.

Customer service is a mixture of knowledge and skills which are learned, not innate. Quality service depends upon a thorough knowledge of the products or services you supply, of the external customers for those products and services, of the systems and procedures of your organization, and of the network of internal customers with whom you work.

An effective programme to improve quality of service is impossible without a sound diagnostic foundation. Diagnostic research has two aspects: the market environment for the organization as a whole, and the things that happen at the interface between the organization and its customers.

Good customer service reflects the whole corporate culture: it depends upon the way that the organization as a whole, from top management downwards, pulls in the same direction, reflecting the corporate mission and clear performance standards, consistent marketing messages, supportive – not obstructive – administrative procedures, and a management style that rewards good customer service behaviour by employees.

This chapter concludes with a review of the positive steps that managers can take in support of the programme; a description of the management briefing cascade; and an outline for an initial 'wake-up' training event.

**NOTES**

1. Robyn Peterson, *Training Needs Analysis in the Workplace*, Kogan Page, 1991.

2. For a more comprehensive discussion of this topic, see: Tony Newby, *Cost-Effective Training – A Manager's Guide*, Kogan Page, 1992.

# *3* Creating the Structure

▷                 SUMMARY                 ◁

This chapter describes the organizational support structure that quality service training will need, including the use of a pool of temporary trainers, the creation of a quality council to oversee the project, and the formation of problem-solving action teams. Reward and recognition options are examined together with the development and monitoring of quality performance standards.

## Introduction

A successful service quality programme rests on a structure that permeates all aspects of organizational life. The components of such a structure are as follows:

- a management-led policy-making body, which may be titled the 'Quality Council';
- a panel of 'temporary trainers' drawn from managerial and supervisory staff, who will be the agents for carrying through the quality training cascade – in particular, training focused upon the 'internal customer' and upon 'quality service' skills;
- a panel of team leaders (typically drawn from junior management) to run problem-solving groups, which may be titled 'Quality Action Teams' or something similar; plus more senior managers who act as mentors to these teams;
- agreed criteria by which to measure changes in performance after training;
- a number of recognition and reward elements, tied to performance criteria.

## Forming a Quality Council

This body takes on responsibility for the overall direction and success of the programme, but not – other than in small organizations – the day-to-day details. The quality council will report directly to the chief executive. All communications about the programme, requests for volunteers, validation of performance measures, presentation of awards and so forth, are done in the name of the council.

The council should include representatives of all levels in the organization, including both senior management and experienced workers. However, in large organizations, the council is likely to grow too large if all departments are represented. It is better that several departments should be represented by one senior manager.

Membership of the quality council will be seen as a high-status activity, but prior status should not be the main criterion when recruiting members. The primary consideration is that all members should be selected on the basis of their enthusiasm for the project and their knowledge of the organization. The debate about whether or not a quality service initiative is needed has to be settled *before* the council is set up. Another essential rule is that there should be no delegation of attendance by members of the council: as soon as people start to send their subordinates, there is a loss of authority, credibility and momentum.

It is likely that the council will need to meet at least once a month in the earlier stages of the programme; later this may become a quarterly review of ongoing activities. The council will often find it useful to create working parties to progress particular elements of the programme. Again, each of these sub-groups should reflect the membership of the full council.

---

### PRACTICAL TIPS

- The quality service programme must be very actively driven by senior line managers: it is not – and must not be seen as – just another training course.
- Limit the quality council to about 10 members at most – and make enthusiasm for quality service the principle criterion for selection.

---

> ## ACTIVITY
>
> **Identify some managers and supervisors at various levels in your organization who you believe would be receptive to the idea of a quality service programme. Conduct informal discussions with each, both to gather diagnostic data about the need and to assess the likely level of support and resourcing for such an initiative.**

## Using Temporary Trainers

A quality service programme creates a large, temporary peak of demand for training resources. One solution is to hire outside suppliers (provided you are getting what you need, not just 'badge engineering'; guidance on use of consultants is given below). A more economical (and often more effective) route is to create your own temporary training force from internal resources. The spin-off benefit is that the organization's managers and supervisors increase their own competence in ways likely to be useful beyond the boundaries of the quality service programme.

In Chapter 2, I described the management cascade for communicating information about the programme in its early stages and subsequently about quality standards, measurement and rewards. Given appropriate training of trainers, a similar result can be achieved for knowledge and skills training within the quality service programme. A small number of managers (to train other managers) and a larger number of supervisors (to train the bulk of employees) will be needed. Volunteers are usually forthcoming, especially when the quality council emphasizes the career development value of this temporary role.

As a rule of thumb, each temporary trainer may be asked to undertake about five identical, short training workshops within a given topic such as internal customer relations, or quality service skills. This minimizes the disruption to their normal duties. There is a trade-off, which has to be resolved in your own local situation, between using the same group of temporary trainers for all training topics (so that each gains more practice) and using different temporary trainers for different stages of the overall programme. The latter is less demanding on the individual in terms of workload and enables more people to gain some training experience, but it also means that temporary trainers may not achieve as great a level of competence. User-friendly working materials need to be provided for these temporary trainers. A selection checklist for recruiting temporary trainers is provided at the end of this section.

The best use of resources may be achieved within each training topic if the more complex, interpersonal skills training is handled by professional trainers (whether internal or consultants) and the more straight forward informational training is handled by the temporary trainers. The latter will, in any event, need to be trained in how to deliver the training. This process should be built around the actual workshop materials that they will use with other employees and you will need to provide them with comprehensive materials: typically a presenter's script plus participants' workbook and possibly video support material. These requirements are discussed in more detail in the respective subject chapters.

There are three training topics within the quality service programme: internal customer relations (Chapter 4), quality service skills (Chapter 6), and team-leader training for quality action teams (Chapter 5). All may be handled through temporary trainers, although it is usually preferable to have quality action team leaders trained by professional trainers.

---

### PRACTICAL TIP

- Don't let people be conscripted into becoming temporary trainers; you must be able to rely on their being keen, committed advocates for the quality service concept.
- A quality service programme isn't a sausage machine: recognize the value of using people's differing strengths and capabilities appropriately.

---

### ACTIVITY

**A selection checklist for recruiting temporary trainers**

1. What evidence do you have that this person is enthusiastic about the quality service programme?

2. Has this person previously taken any steps to train the staff he or she supervises?

3. What career benefit does this person anticipate from becoming a part-time temporary trainer?

4. What problem is this training role likely to create for this individual's usual work duties?

5. Does this person feel comfortable with the idea of standing up in front of a group and lecturing?

6. Does this person feel comfortable with the idea of helping a group to practise interpersonal skills?

## Using External Consultants

Good consultants will offer specialist expertise on quality service issues – and will practise in their relationships with your organization the skills they are recommending you acquire. Consultants can also offer a degree of independence which gives greater objectivity when reviewing what is happening in your organization. They should be free from the history and prejudgments that have accumulated, sometimes over decades, in your own organization. An effective consultancy assignment has much in common with an effective training design: establishing needs and developing appropriate responses.

The greatest risks of consultancy not working out arise where:

- the consultant's claim to expertise is unjustified;
- there is a mismatch of expectations, due to inadequate initial diagnostic work;
- the client has a goal which is being kept from the consultant (clients using consultants to fire their bullets for them);
- the client wants to be seen to be 'doing something' without a commitment to real change;
- the consultant's diagnosis is too accurate for comfort and the organization closes ranks to protect the status quo;
- consultants make promises that they cannot deliver, breach confidentiality, or over-charge;
- the consultancy provides a service that is all presentation and no substance (a particular risk where the salesperson and the consultant who delivers the service are different people).

## Structuring The Quality Action Teams

In parallel with the structure of temporary trainers, there needs to be a separate structure for quality action teams (QATs) because of the wide application and long-term continuation of this element of the programme. There are four elements to this structure: the steering group, mentors, coordinators, and team leaders.

The QAT steering group, reporting in to the quality council, has oversight of all quality action teams, coordinates projects that may overlap, conflict with, or duplicate others, as well as providing a forum for review of the ideas generated by quality action teams. It is essential to provide a process for managing rejected ideas, to prevent loss of motivation by teams. The steering group is composed of representatives of team leaders, mentors and senior managers.

### Mentors

Mentors are middle or senior managers who act as an informal sounding-board, guide, and friend to two or three quality action teams. Mentors need to be willing to stand back and let the teams get on with their task. They do not take part in the team meetings, but provide support and advice on request.

### Coordinators

A coordinator has a liaison and trouble-shooting role between all parts of the quality action team programme; the role is likely to be undertaken by a professional trainer (in large organizations, more than one may be needed). The coordinator reports to the QAT steering group.

### Team Leaders

QAT team leaders may be selected both from supervisors and from amongst experienced workers. The team leader should not be much more senior than the members of the team; otherwise, there tends to be too much hierarchical deference, which impedes open and creative problem-solving. Teams will consist of four to eight people, generally drawn from the same area of work, although occasionally there will also be value in cross-departmental teams. The role of team leader combines elements of training, facilitation of group discussions, and team leadership. It offers a valuable test-bed for potential supervisors. Guidance on selection and training is given in Chapter 5.

## Reward And Recognition Options

As well as the training itself and post-training reinforcement by line managers there may be value in creating a system of formal recognition and/or rewards for employees who perform to (or exceed) measured standards. The basic distinction is between 'rewards' such as one-off cash payments, additional increments on salary scales and the like, and 'recognition' awards which have status but not pecuniary value. Examples of recognition awards include 'employee of the month', a 'quality achievers' dinner dance, publicity for quality innovations, and the opportunity for the very best proposals from quality action teams to be presented by the originating team to the top management of the organization.

It may be argued that the 'recognition' route is both more effective than the 'reward' one and usually less expensive. The argument against use of rewards is that employees are already paid to do their jobs and ought not to receive additional payments for doing their jobs properly. Conversely, recognition of those who achieve results beyond the norm is

41

fully justified and the associated status has longer-lasting motivational impact. The individual continues to 'live up to' an enhanced personal identity, long after an award of cash or goods would have been consumed and forgotten.

All rewards and recognition should be based upon well-defined measurable outputs that relate directly to the purposes for which the organization exits. They should not be rewards for input: if people are 'trying hard' but there is no measurable output, then the quality programme has been misconceived. There are two ways to measure output achievements: the first uses such measures as time, quality, cost and quantity, incorporated into performance standards and applied to the services that the organization delivers to its customers. Such improvements in output measures should link back into the objectives of the quality service training that has been provided.

It is a good rule not to make recognition awards or pecuniary rewards too exclusive or highly competitive. It is better to position them as something that is presented for attaining a high, but realistic, level of performance, and therefore attainable by everyone. In the earlier stages of the programme awards may be distributed more freely but as average performance standards rise it may become necessary to 'move the goalposts' by raising the target level of good performance.

An essential element of both reward and recognition schemes is publicity: principally internally, but also as useful PR targeted on external customers. A quality of service newsletter can be set up to provide information about the programme as a whole and also to highlight specific achievements by teams or individuals.

The second approach to measurement is to use subjective opinion data from internal and external customers. A composite index of service quality can be put together using data collected from several sources. The weighting given to different sources and measures is a matter of choice by your organization; there is no set formula. As an example, the index might be made up as follows:

- external customer opinions applied to the whole organization, collected by postal or telephone survey (25 per cent);
- internal customer opinions applied to each department or section, collected by postal survey or interview (15 per cent);
- mystery phone caller data (simulating external or internal customer enquiries) collected for individual departments or sections (15 per cent);
- quality rating of the ideas generated by quality action teams, allocated to departments or sections, carried out by the QAT

coordinator on behalf of the quality council (15 per cent);
- achievement of performance standards applied to the whole department, measured by line managers (usually quarterly) (20 per cent for corporate standards; 10 per cent for departmental).

## Quality Standards

Standards provide three key elements in the quality service system:

1. Yardsticks by which the quality of service can be measured – yardsticks which must reflect the levels of expectation that other organizations are creating amongst your own customers.
2. Guidance on how particular elements of quality service are to be delivered in day-to-day work: standards focus upon practical aspects of service to external and internal customers.
3. A motivational boost to the quality programme which arises because standards *must* be observed by everyone, up to the chief executive, thereby obviating the 'us and them' divisiveness of many change programmes.

Four processes are involved: developing standards; putting them in place in the organization; monitoring at regular intervals whether performance matches standards; and rewards or recognition of achievement.

## Developing Standards

Standards should emerge from the initial diagnostic research that underpins the quality service programme. Standards may be developed by:

- managers and personnel specialists who analyse job tasks and determine what the appropriate standard of performance should be;
- trainers who establish standards as a part of training in job skills;
- employees themselves, typically when they are active in quality action teams or similar groups;
- external consultants who are managing your quality programme.

Quality standards are usually measured in terms of task-time, output quantity, cost-saving, output quality (eg, absence of errors) and the like. Standards should not be unduly weighted by process measures rather than output measures. Two levels of standard may need to be developed: corporate standards which apply to everyone; and local or departmental standards which are specific to one part of the enterprise. It is a good working rule to keep the number of standards as low as possible: 20 to 30 standards grouped into theme clusters is the maximum; in the earlier stages of the project, 15 or so is a desirable maximum number for workers and managers to keep track of.

It is likely that the topics for standards that emerge from diagnostic research will fall into logical themes or context groupings. You should select groupings that make sense for your own situation, rather than automatically adopt schemes in use elsewhere. Examples of groupings for standards are as follows.

*Example 1*

- standards relating to the organization's product;
- standards relating to how people within the organization work together;
- standards relating to how employees relate to customers;
- standards relating to policies and administrative procedures;
- standards relating to the physical environment within which services are delivered.

*Example 2*

- standards relating to how each employee manages the work throughput;
- standards relating to internal communications;
- standards relating to the management of each individual's and/or section's work-space;
- standards relating to each employee's work-related learning activities.

## Examples of Performance Standards

Many quality service problems are similar in a great many organizations and therefore, once your diagnostic research has identified the areas of concern, you may be able to take a short-cut by adapting and borrowing standards that are in use elsewhere. However, don't lose sight of the need to fine-tune other organizations' standards; be firm in rejecting those that are inappropriate to your situation and remember that there will always be some standards that are unique to the context in which you work. Some examples of fairly frequently-encountered standards follow:

*Example 1*
Right first time – tasks (or parts of tasks) are completed correctly, so that work does not have to be returned for corrective action.

*Example 2*

When something is promised to an internal or external customer, the promise must be realistic, it must be kept, and any unforeseen and unavoidable delays must be notified.

*Example 3*

When you 'inherit' errors that have been passed on from elsewhere in the organization, you will not pass those errors on to others (this may require that you return the incorrect work, or that you refer it to your supervisor or manager).

*Example 4*

All written work must be clear and understandable (this may require that your organization agrees a set of style rules for all documents and correspondence, covering such matters as jargon, sentence complexity, obligation to give clear explanations, and the like).

*Example 5*

Records, correspondence and files should be left in a state such that they could be easily dealt with by someone other than the person who normally handles those items.

## Putting Standards In Place

Standards need to be a management-driven rather than a trainer-driven initiative. The management cascade is a good way to disseminate information about the standards system and to explain to each level in the organization how standards will be implemented, what the measurement process will be and how measurement ties into rewards.

## Auditing Achievement of Standards

Regular monitoring is needed to determine whether performance matches standards, both at an individual and at a sectional or departmental level. This process may be integrated with regular appraisal sessions or be treated as a separate activity. A quarterly review is very desirable, though operational constraints may make six-month intervals necessary. If at all possible, aim for shorter intervals in the earlier stages of the quality programme and extend the intervals as the system becomes routinely established .

A simple scoring matrix can be developed which enables a manager to review the performance of each standard against a five-point scale:

0 = Total failure to attain standard
1 = Partial failure
2 = Adequate achievement of standard
3 = Achievement of standard well above the adequacy level
4 = Excellence in performing to the standard.

Scores can be aggregated for individuals and for sections, as the basis both of remedial action (through training and/or management supervision) and of rewards, recognition, or even sanctions.

It is essential to the credibility of the standards operation that the quality council formally monitors the scoring process in order to make compensatory adjustments for the (usually small) proportion of managers and supervisors who systematically score over-generously or over-meanly.

## Cash Awards

Initially, it is likely to ease the introduction of performance standards if one-off cash awards are made for achievement of an agreed level of scoring on standards. Subsequently, routine salary increments may be made conditional upon achievement of specified levels of standards.

## Training In The Use Of Standards

A training pack should be prepared for the managers and supervisors involved in the information cascade. The pack will consist of speaker's notes, overhead projector slides, and exercise material. Examples of trainer's notes are given in Figures 3.1 and 3.2

# Chapter Review

This chapter has outlined the organizational support structure for quality service training: a quality council to oversee the project; the use of a pool of temporary trainers; the formation of problem-solving quality action teams; and the development and monitoring of quality performance standards linked to rewards and recognition. The importance of rewarding measurable outputs rather than input processes has been emphasized.

1. You may find it useful to prepare flipchart sheets which list the quality standards using a short phrase that conveys the essence of that standard. The full listing of the relevant standards is provided on the handout sheet. Issue the handout when you have finished running through the list, so that you keep their attention on what you are saying.

2. Run through the list of standards fairly briskly, emphasizing the ways in which achievement of each will prevent complaints and contribute to quality service. Also make the point that corporate standards are a base for good service, but do not encompass the whole of it – one purpose of today's workshop is to take participants beyond that minimum level and help them develop superior skills. Comment also that standards can be a way of focusing upon whether or not systems, procedures, rules, etc. are in fact customer-friendly. Where they are not, there may be opportunities through the quality action teams to change things for the better.

3. Avoid getting into any debate about the rights and wrongs of having standards, or any questions about the fairness or otherwise of the standards assessment process. These are matters for the participants to discuss with their own line supervisors.

4. Use the short exercise to get participants to think about what corporate standards mean for quality service in their own jobs. Issue the exercise sheet.

**Figure 3.1** *Trainer's notes for information about corporate and departmental standards*

For each of the quality standards listed below, write down how that standard would apply to the job you yourself do. You may find it useful afterwards to talk to your supervisor about the answers you have written down – and about their implications for how work gets done in your part of the organization.

Example 2: When something is promised to an internal or external customer, the promise must be realistic, it must be kept, and any unforeseen and unavoidable delays must be notified.

How Example 2 applies to my work:

etc. …

**Figure 3.2** *Exercise on corporate and departmental standards*

# 4 Strengthening the Internal Customer Chain

▷ SUMMARY ◁

This chapter introduces the concept of the internal customer service chain which forms an essential foundation if quality service is to be delivered to external customers. The role of an internal customer working party to steer this element of the programme is described.

Learning aims that underpin the design of an internal customer workshop are suggested, addressing in particular such questions as 'Does everybody really have customers?', 'Who are our internal customers?' and 'How do we work together more effectively?'. The training of temporary trainers and the development of trainers' notes, participants' workbooks and take-away reference materials are described, with examples of exercises and guidance on the use of video and case studies.

## Introduction

In order to deliver quality service to the customers for whom the organization primarily exists, it is necessary first to put your own house in order. In other words, the quality of service within the organization must match the quality that you aspire to deliver externally. The way to tackle this requirement is through an 'internal customer' element within the overall service quality programme.

## What is An Internal Customer?

The concept is based upon the fact that *everybody* in an organization either directly serves customers or helps colleagues (their internal customers) who form a chain of internal customer service within the organization that eventually interfaces with an external customer. The quality of that external customer relationship depends not only on what happens at the point of contact, but also on what has already happened all the way along the internal customer chain.

The idea of an internal customer chain is fine, so long as there are no weak links. There are few problems when everyone pulls in the same direction. However, it is surprisingly common to encounter individuals, sections and even whole departments, who believe that they are so remote from 'real' customers that quality of service cannot possibly be an issue for them. Since this means that they are contributing nothing to the organization's outputs, the most economical solution is to allow such individuals or departments to make their non-contribution elsewhere.

Of course, the reality is that these people are often contributing essential inputs to the organization but simply do not recognize that their inputs have a bearing on the service delivered to external customers.

An even more frequently-encountered set of problems in the internal customer service system relates to the interface between one part of the organization and another – problems of communication (very typical of head office/branch conflicts); of the quality of work passed on (where different people handle different stages of a document, for instance); of entrenched negative views ('us and them' barriers) created by different perceptions of job priorities (typically between sales and administration, between marketing and manufacturing and between computer departments and computer users).

This chapter describes how you can play a positive role in making good internal customer service the norm. An effective training workshop offers employees the opportunity to see themselves as part of the solution, rather than part of the problem. It has the bonus that it is more fun to work in an organization with a problem-solving culture than one where problems are perpetuated and made an excuse for finger-pointing.

## Diagnostic foundations

Your starting point in designing the internal customer training should, of course, be the preliminary research into quality service problems that underpins your whole programme. This research is likely to have yielded plenty of examples of internal customer issues that will shape the direction of your training and which will provide convincing material (when made anonymous) for case studies and exercises.

If you run some sort of 'quality wake-up' event at the very beginning of the programme, you can collect comments from participants that will provide another fertile source of internal customer concerns. A simple feedback form such as Figure 4.1 should gather the data you need.

List below as many examples that you can think of where things have not been done as well as they could have been. For example, in the way that the customers who buy our goods or services are treated; in the ways that one part of this organization works with any other part; in individual communications; in a lack of knowledge or skills training that would enable people to do the job better; or anything else that you feel may affect the quality of service we provide.

For each example you give, try to be specific and give details about what happened, how people reacted, and what the consequence was.

**Figure 4.1** *Employee concerns about service quality (for use at initial 'quality wake-up' event)*

## The Internal Customer Working Party

The next step is to form a working party, under the umbrella of the quality council, that will be responsible for the design and implementation of the internal customer elements of the quality programme. Within the working party there needs to be a mix of not only expertise and authority levels but – of equal importance – a mix that represents different steps in the internal customer chain. This is not to say that every department or section must be represented: that is just a recipe for creating a talking shop.

There *must* be representation of any parts of the organization that are known to have particularly acute mutual difficulties (eg, head office and branch, or sales and administration, or computer department and computer users, etc.). There should also be representation of technical or professional specialists (as permanent or occasional members) to ensure that the details are right, and of any external training consultants who are involved in the design and development.

The role of the working party is to steer the design (ensuring that key issues are included), to manage the implementation (ensuring resourcing), and to legitimize the process (on the one hand, by authority derived from the quality council; on the other, by communicating the purposes of the internal customer training via the management cascade). The working party should approve the training design and content, but will not usually write the material – a recipe for confusion. (A possible exception to this rule may be the small organization with limited resources, where preparation tasks have to be spread around the members of the working party). In general, the detailed preparatory work will be carried out by the training department, or by external consultants working to their briefing.

---

### PRACTICAL TIPS

- There *must* be representation of any parts of the organization that are known to have mutually poor internal customer relations.
- The working party should act as the guardian of programme integrity and its advocate within the organization, but should resist the temptations of detailed preparatory work.

---

## Setting Learning Aims

The aims should emerge from the diagnostic data and the examples given below are just examples, not a definitive or universal list.

*Example 1.* To understand the nature and significance of internal customer service quality

This is concerned with employees' understanding of the ways in which the various parts of the organization fit together to provide the products and service that keep customers coming back with repeat business.

*Example 2.* To increase cooperative behaviour between department 'A' and department 'B'

Note that this is a more useful, positive formulation of the negatively-stated objective 'To reduce stereotyped and hostile perceptions between department "A" and department "B"', the 'us and them' syndrome. Example 2 puts the emphasis on the new behaviours that you want to see happening, rather than on the old ones you wish to eliminate.

*Example 3.* To learn to use a problem-solving approach to all internal customer service issues

This is the kind of objective that may emerge from a diagnosed problem of responsibility for problem-solving being passed to others, who are alleged to be the source of the problem. It lends itself to co-operative, cross-departmental pursuit of solutions, rather than the negative process of shifting blame; to a search for ways the individual *can* do things, rather than for the reasons to put things off, or to pass the buck.

*Example 4.* To increase knowledge of the various functions within the organization, including the way in which these form links in an internal customer quality service chain

The premise here is that diagnostic research often shows ignorance of other parts of the organization's work to be an issue; it can be the case that many employees do not understand how their own work dovetails into the work of other sections and thus do not understand how their own errors and omissions undermine the internal customer chain.

*Example 5.* To reinforce the performance standards and the quality action team elements of the service quality programme

This aim reflects the interdependency and mutual reinforcement of the different parts of the quality service training programme. For example, amongst the performance standards to be introduced, there should be some that create standards for internal customer quality. Amongst the problems that quality action teams address, some (typically, many) will relate to internal customer issues.

---

### PRACTICAL TIPS

- The aims of internal customer training must be grounded in your diagnostic research, not in textbook models.
- Try never to lose sight of the inter-connections between *all* the parts of the quality service programme: internal customer, performance standards, service skills, action teams, manager involvement.

---

## Designing the Internal Customer Training Workshop

There are several components that may need to be provided for this workshop:

- Trainers' notes and visual aids (for running the workshop – particularly important if temporary trainers are to be employed).
- Training of trainers workshop.
- Participants' materials (exercises and handout notes used during the event).
- Video material integrated with the workshop objectives and other content (purpose-made or hired).
- Participants' take-away materials (factual information that is most effectively handled by individual reading following the workshop).

### Trainers' Notes and Visual Aids

The trainers' notes are best laid out in well-spaced text, using a large typeface for easy reference during training sessions, and may be contained in a loose-leaf binder. There must be clear cross-references to separate exercises, handouts to be issued to participants, times at which the video (if any) is to be used, and to overhead projector slides linked to the text.

The trainers' notes can start off with general introductory comments and then provide session-by-session 'key points' guidelines. Additional help in using the material should come from attendance at training of trainers workshops. It is helpful – especially to temporary trainers – for each of the sessional notes to follow a standard format. This helps to achieve a consistent quality in the training as well as providing a check that no important element of the training design has been missed. A standardized format is provided in Figure 4.2.

---

- Introductory comments by the trainer, bridging from the previous activity.
- Statement of the formal learning objective(s) that relate to that session.
- Presentation to the audience (factual information, description and illustration of skills, and so on), comprising:
    - key points summary of training inputs;
    - lead-in remarks for activities ('Why we're doing this exercise'; 'What steps you should follow').
- Activities by trainees connecting learning points to trainees' own work experience (questions, discussion, practice of skills, paper-based exercises, and so on).
- Key points debriefing of the session (trigger questions to use; making the transfer to work; summary review of learning points).
- Lead-in remarks for the next session.

---

**Figure 4.2** *Checklist for trainer's notes*

In similar fashion, a standard format can be adopted for each practical exercise, as illustrated in Figure 4.3.

---

- Explanation of 'Why we're doing this exercise'.
- Description of the steps the participants should follow, including any division of trainees into sub-groups as well as introduction of any support materials (such as behaviour observation checklists, discussed in Chapter 6).
- Running the exercise (including any interim reviews, correction of errors, etc. as appropriate).
- Whole group ('plenary') debriefing of the exercise, including preparation by the trainer of trigger questions to provoke debate, reinforce learning and encourage transfer of new knowledge and skills into the trainees' work.

---

**Figure 4.3** *Checklist for format of practical exercises*

The trainers' notes do not as a rule provide a word-for-word script: experienced trainers usually like to use their own style and choice of words and even temporary trainers should not be perceived to be reading from a script.

It is very important where trainers personalize the material that key points are not watered down and that the trainer's choice of language, tone of voice, body language, etc. all convey a clear commitment to the purpose of the workshop. Any reservations about the training must be resolved before the trainer gets in front of a workshop group.

---

### PRACTICAL TIPS

- Make the trainers' notes for presentations and exercises in each session follow a standard format.
- Vigorously weed out any trainer, temporary or permanent, who is half-hearted about the aims of the quality service programme.

---

## Training of Trainers Workshop

Experienced trainers still need to familiarize themselves with new material. Temporary trainers have this need superimposed on a probable need to develop their basic training skills. Their credibility is greatly enhanced when they can run the workshop without constant reference to notes or prompt cards, though these should certainly be kept available for emergencies – even experienced trainers can dry up sometimes. However, rather than go through a full-blown process of trainer-training with them, it is much more economical to carry out a limited form of trainer-training wholly within the framework of practising to deliver the internal customer module. Basic topics such as presentation, running exercises, giving feedback to trainees and the like can be offered using the materials which the temporary trainers will subsequently deliver.

Figure 4.4 shows an example of notes for temporary trainers on how to open a training event; Figure 4.5 illustrates training of trainers notes on presenting a training session.

1. The opening session sets the tone for what follows. Get housekeeping issues out of the way quickly so that they do not intrude later into the momentum of the event. 'Housekeeping' issues are the administrative details like:

- mealtimes;
- fire alarms;
- name 'tents' (if you do not know them all personally);
- toilets;
- the time that hotel rooms have to be vacated, or premises locked up (as appropriate).

2. After welcoming trainees, get to the point of why they are there:

- state the formal objectives of the event (it is often helpful to have these ready on a prepared flipchart or slide);
- link this event with preceding activities in the organization;
- emphasize your expectation that trainees will learn something useful (they are not here for rest and recreation) – the event is not about theory or good intentions but about practical applications back at work;
- explain how this training event relates to the quality service programme and why the latter is so important to the future of the organization;
- describe how the group will be working – the style of the event, the type of activities and your own anticipation of lively discussion and active contributions by group members.

3. Invite questions about the broad purpose of the training event – but defer any detailed specifics until the relevant session. This is definitely not the time to start debating what should or should not be included in the timetable.

4. Respond appropriately to anyone who (rightly or wrongly) feels that he or she ought not to be attending this particular event. Depending upon the individual, your response may range from 'Wait and see how the event unfolds, before you judge it', through to 'I agree that you should not be here until you have discussed your learning needs with your line manager'.

**Figure 4.4** *Opening a training event*

1. Every trainee should be able to feel that he or she can make a positive contribution. Big themes tend to overwhelm people ('That problem is too big for me to deal with'). It is worth emphasizing that most changes come about from large numbers of small improvements of the kind that they can themselves make.

2. A list of key points written onto index cards is easier to work with – and makes your presentation sound more natural – than a fully-written-out script.

3. Experienced presenters like to use their own style and choice of words. You can give depth to your presentation with *relevant* illustrations drawn from your own experience, but avoid stories that put down other people. When personalizing material be sure that the key learning points are not omitted.

4. Remember that preaching at people does not work: it is the process of applying new knowledge and skills to the individual's job that makes the difference. Effective training is that training which helps the trainee to translate the message into practice.

5. Beware of humour: it often backfires, either immediately or after the event. Totally avoid jokes about race, religion, politics, ill-health, death or customers.

6. Your choice of language, tone of voice, body language, all must convey your commitment to the purposes of the training. Watch out too for signs that you may be losing part (or all) of your audience. It is helpful to pause every ten minutes or so to check their understanding and to invite questions.

7. Never forget that the average span of attention is about 20 minutes and 80 per cent of a lecture is forgotten within 24 hours unless your inputs are reinforced by practice. Ensure there are frequent changes of activity, eg, from listening to you, to discussing how your points apply in their job, or to doing a practical exercise or a role play.

**Figure 4.5** *Making training presentations*

## Participants' Materials

These consist of the practical exercises and the reference notes for each participant. It is more likely that the material will be retained by employees and used as a reference source if it is attractively presented and securely bound. It does not need to be a super-glossy item: a printed cover and comb-binding are perfectly satisfactory.

An example of the integration of the trainers' notes and the participants', workbook is given by Figures 4.6 (Trainer's notes) and 4.7 (Participants' materials).

*Notes to trainer:* It is predictable that any group attending a training event concerned with internal customer relations will have a fund of horror stories, resentments, etc. which they are poised to unload (usually at an inconvenient or inappropriate moment). Exercise 1 seeks to preempt this by making it OK for people to air their prejudices and grievances about other departments. The process should make participants more receptive to the messages of the following sessions. It also provides material that can be worked on as the workshop develops.

*Objectives:* (Example 1 from p. 52) To understand the nature and significance of internal customer service quality.

*Trainer input:*

1. The purpose of this activity is to give you all a chance to share some of your experiences to date of what can go wrong with our goal of all working together to provide excellent customer service.

2. Issue the Exercise 1 introduction and the exercise sheet.

3. I'd like you to start off working on your own – take three or four minutes to jot down brief notes about incidents you've experienced personally, things that have made it harder for you to do your job properly:

- it may be things that other people do, but you'd rather they didn't;
- it may be things that you'd like other people to do differently;
- it may be things that others don't do, but it would help if they did.

4. When you've finished, find a partner who doesn't work in your own section. Discuss your lists – are you suffering from similar problems? Between you, decide which items on your lists might be improvable. Tick the yes or no columns on the sheet. What would be the benefits both to yourself and to this organization if the potential improvements that you have identified could be realized?

You've got about five minutes in which to complete this. Is it clear what I'm asking you to do?

5. After about five minutes call the group together again:

- ask for examples of 'improvables'. It may be worth flipcharting these to feed important points back to the quality council;
- ask for a few examples of 'unimprovables': list them, but don't at this stage get into debate about whether or not they really are unimprovable – there are better opportunities later.
- explore whether there are common features. Comment that these are similar to many of the issues now being tackled by quality action teams made up of people very similar to your present audience – but don't sidetrack into specifics.

6. Lead into the next session: we've started to explore the 'them and us' attitude for ourselves. Now let's look at the whole picture – the service chain all the way from the external, paying customer back through the branches and head office departments and then out again to the customer.

**Figure 4.6** *Trainer's sessional notes for Exercise 1: 'Them!'*

Even though you may want to change things, you (and your colleagues) do not start off with a clean sheet. There is often a history of greater or lesser frictions which occurred for reasons that – at the time – seemed valid, but which now live on as a legacy of touchiness or distrust. This is a chance to get off your chest some of the irritations you feel from time to time about the acts and omissions of other sections, Head office departments, and branches – all those 'thems' who complicate our lives.

Use the 'Review Sheet' (following) to make brief notes about any incidents that you personally have experienced where colleagues have failed to give you the kind of service that you should get as their internal customer – incidents that have made it harder for you to do your job properly. Start off working on your own. List anything that adversely affects your work:

- things that others do (but you'd rather they didn't);
- things that others do (that you'd like them to do differently);
- things other people don't do (but it would help if they did).

Note who it is that is causing you problems.

When you've finished your list find a partner – ideally someone who doesn't work in your own section or department, because you want to get a fresh perspective on the problems. Talk through your list and your partner's list:

- are you suffering from similar problems (or similar kinds of people)?
- how much are the problems a matter of where you happen to be standing at the time?
- is one person's 'problem' another person's 'correct way to do things'?
- are the problems being magnified simply because you don't know the individuals you are dealing with (especially over the telephone) so you tend to assume the worst of them?
- are there misunderstandings because you don't really know what other departments do (or are permitted to do)?
- which items on your lists ought – at least in principle – to be improvable?
- what could be the benefits to either the organization or yourselves if these improvements were made?
- what would it take to achieve each of those improvements?

Go back over your 'yeses' and discuss with your partner what the benefits of an improvement might add up to – both for yourself and for the organization as a whole. Lastly, jot down ideas for what it might take to get changes made.

*Exercise 1 Review Sheet*

| Who 'Them' is | Their Acts and Omissions | Improvable | | Benefits from Improvement | What it Would Take |
|---|---|---|---|---|---|
| | | Yes | No | | |
| | | | | | |

**Figure 4.7** *Exercise 1 for participants: 'Them!'*

## Using Films and Video

Video can add considerable impact to training sessions: providing drama-tized illustrations of 'problem' situations; demonstrating appropriate use of service skills; acting as a trigger to group discussion. However, the credibility of the service quality programme can be seriously damaged if the video material is unsuitable or inadequate.

Ready-made films are often seen as good value in training, especially when hire charges are compared to the production cost of a company-specific video, but there are several essential questions to ask before using such material:

- is it relevant to the training need you are addressing?
- is there anything in the film that may undermine the quality service message?
- what will people be asked to do as well as watching the film?

One of the problems with training films or videos is that they often *nearly* make the point you want, but actually deal with something a bit different, or else they put the learning point into a context that may be difficult for your people to relate to. Film may also be a problem simply because of its visual impact: the quality of the acting and the entertainment value may overwhelm the learning issues.

Difficulties may arise because the film relates to a different kind of industry, or organizational culture. Trainees can take a seemingly per-verse delight in finding things in films that 'aren't the way we do it here' and use this as an excuse to reject all other messages, however relevant, that it contains.

Films are too often presented as if the act of viewing them was the whole training process. However, video is a passive training medium (not to be used after a heavy lunch!). A video or film needs to be supple-mented by activities which involve the viewers. A useful support tech-nique is the video review sheet which asks questions about key elements of the film: an example of a review sheet is given in Figure 4.8. The answers form the basis for discussions of potential applications of learn-ing points to trainees' jobs. Always make sure that you have watched the film beforehand and have made a list of the learning points that you want people to take away from it.

If you are commissioning video material, use a trigger format of short, self-contained episodes rather than a single continuous storyline. If you are hiring video material, try, whenever practicable, to show it in short episodes rather than continuously (some films just do not lend them-selves to this treatment – so consider whether they really meet your needs). The point of breaking up the film is to allow you to conduct practical exercises, group discussions and so forth.

---

Instructions:

Here are a few questions to help focus your attention on the key issues in the video. Take a quick look at the list before the video is switched on and when it's finished write in your answers. Don't spoil your enjoyment of the video by trying to write in the answers as it is being shown – this isn't a test!

1. What is the customer in the first episode annoyed about?

2. If Jane had not retrieved the situation, how many different groups of people with whom that customer is likely to have contact might have got to hear about the organization's error?

3. What is a customer worth to your organization over a typical life-span?

4. List five things that Jane did correctly in response to the situation:

5. List three good things that Bob does to resolve Mr Gray's problem:

6. List as many things as you can think of that are done badly by the angry clerk in the final scene.

---

**Figure 4.8** *Example of a video review sheet for one episode of a customer service video*

## Participants' Take-Away Materials

The internal customer workshop should be used as an opportunity to increase interpersonal skills and problem-solving capabilities; it is a wasted opportunity to use it for 'information-dumping'. There is likely to be quite a lot of information about the organization that needs to be transmitted to employees as part of the internal customer training, but there are more cost-effective ways to do this than by taking up workshop time.

One option is to create an internal 'quality services' newsletter, covering matters within the whole programme. Another solution is to provide workshop participants with 'take-away' packs of essential information, to be read later and retained for reference. The content of such a pack will vary from one enterprise to another; the following is simply an example, not a definitive list:

**Information Pack Contents (Internal Customer Relations):**
1. Visual representation of a typical 'Customer Service Chain' in the XYZ Organization

2. 'This is XYZ Organization …'
- descriptions of each department's functions;
- history of the organization;
- key personalities.

It may be useful to distinguish between those departments that are mainly internally-focused and those mainly externally-focused; eg:

*Mainly internal customer-facing*
- Personnel
- Training
- Investment Planning
- Accountants
- Information Technology

*Mainly external customer-facing*
- Branch Sales Offices
- Sales
- Marketing
- Customer Administration

3. Introduction to performance standards relating to internal customers

4. A summary note about quality service to internal customers, eg:
- Courtesy in verbal and written communications.
- Knowing where your job fits in the service chain.
- Working cooperatively with colleagues.
- Meeting corporate and departmental standards.
- Clear and accurate communication.
- Prevention rather than cure.
- Prompt and effective resolution of problems.
- Continuous, small improvements.

## Content of the Internal Customer Workshop

The main emphasis of the workshop is upon the idea of the customer service chain – in which everyone is a link – and this can be illustrated by a training sequence based upon a typical customer transaction, following it all the way through the organization. The details of training content will be determined by learning objectives based upon the diagnostic research and will reflect the culture, economic situation and purposes of the organization.

That said, there are a number of themes that commonly appear when internal customer relations are at issue:

- stereotyped perceptions between different parts of the organization;
- a need for problem-solving rather than blaming behaviours;
- inadequate understanding of the functions and interdependence of each department and section of the organization;
- widespread failure by individuals to identify their position and role within the chain of service;
- a need to improve the quality of work passed to colleagues in the internal service chain.

Given such typical themes, a half-day workshop might be timetabled as in Figure 4.9.

| Duration of session (*minutes*) | Session content |
|---|---|
| 10 | Introduction |
| 30 | Exercise to reduce 'us and them' stereotyping |
| 40 | Showing of 'Internal Customer' video, with individual completion of video review sheet and group discussion of key messages from the video |
| 20 | Tea/coffee break |
| 15 | Exercise on 'Mapping My Customer Network' |
| 35 | Exercise on internal customer problem-solving |
| 35 | Exercise on passing work to colleagues |
| 20 | Personal action planning plus plenary feedback |
| 10 | Introduction of 'take-away' package |
| 15 | Re-run of video |

*Total:* 3 hours 50 minutes

**Figure 4.9** *Internal customer workshop timetable*

The 'us and them' exercise has already been illustrated, and the use of video discussed. Outline examples of the other exercises are given as follows:

- Figure 4.10: to develop individual understanding of the internal customer chain;
- Figure 4.11: internal customer problem-solving;
- Figure 4.12: passing work to colleagues.

*Instructions:*

Think of your network as a series of inputs and outputs, with yourself at the centre. Various things get passed to you (information, work tasks, queries, etc.) and you in turn pass various things on to others in the chain, or else directly to external customers.

Use the chart (following) to list who is in your internal customer network – and what it is that gets passed along the service chain. So far as you are able, write in the names of the actual people you deal with. Only use a job title or general description if you don't know their names or if there are a lot of people in the same category (eg, 'sales assistants'). You may find it helpful to talk to your supervisor about this. There is space for up to four inputs and four outputs. You can adjust these numbers to match your own particular situation.

When you have completed the chart, go on to the improvements sheet that follows. For each of your inputs and outputs, make brief notes on what might improve the way that link in the chain could be handled, by others and by yourself. Note that most solutions require quite small adjustments in the way people do their jobs – it's not the blockbuster projects, but close attention to small details that adds up to quality of service.

*Mapping your place in the internal customer chain*

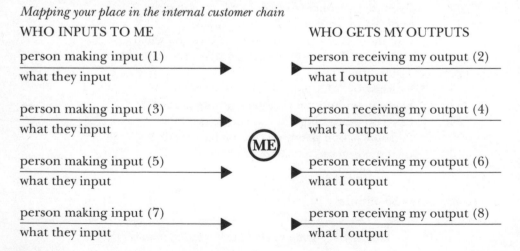

64

*Improvements sheet (inputs)*

| Input number | Changes that would help me to do my job more effectively | What might I be able to do to help make that happen? |
|---|---|---|
| 1. | | |
| etc | | |
| | | |

*Improvements sheet (outputs)*

| Output number | Changes that would help others do their jobs more effectively | What could I do to make that happen? |
|---|---|---|
| 1. | | |
| etc. | | |
| | | |

Improvements Sheet: Supervisor's Inputs

Discuss your improvement sheets with your supervisor or manager. Make a note here of the comments and suggestions that you receive:

**Figure 4.10** *Mapping your place in the internal customer chain*

*Instructions:*

At some time, you've probably experienced shortfalls in our internal customer service. But it's worth reflecting that sometimes we ourselves may be the 'them' causing the upset. The purpose of this activity is to give you a feel for what it's like to be in some internal customer situations that crop up outside your own area of work.

Form groups of about four people to work on one of the case studies provided. This should be a case which relates to a situation outside your own work. Read the case description and individually complete the work sheet. Then, in the group, compare your reactions and proposed solutions, and make notes of additional useful ideas that come from other members of the group.

*Internal customer problem-solving: work sheet*

1. If I were the person in this situation, how would I feel about it?

2. What would I want to do about the situation?

3. What help, support or information might I need?

4. What could I do to stop this situation recurring?

**Figure 4.11** *Internal customer problem-solving*

Case studies are a useful training tool to assist people to learn about the *process* of problem-solving; whether or not people get to the 'right' answer is neither here nor there. They enable people to identify hidden elements of the problem-solving process and to practise appropriate skills, in particular:

- to recognize (and challenge) unquestioned assumptions, values and attitudes held by the parties to the process;
- to analyse the available information and draw out conclusions and implications from the facts;
- to arrive – by one means or another – at decisions.

De-briefing of case studies should follow this pattern:

- recap on the purpose of the exercise;
- use open-ended questions to trigger debate on the ways in which the groups(s) tackled the task;
- remind the group of any occasions where their group process (their interpersonal behaviour) got in the way of the formal (problem-solving) task;
- encourage connections between what happened in the exercise and the 'real world' of the trainees' own jobs, noting that most solutions

involve very modest changes in the way people do their jobs – 'quality' comes from close attention to important small details;

- summarize the main learning points, especially the value of problem solving rather than whingeing, the value of working with colleagues and the differences between individual and group solutions.

Case studies should err on the side of simplicity. There is no virtue in complicated case studies with masses of data to be analysed – *unless* that reflects the specific training objectives. The main purpose of a case is to trigger an experience of a process of working in a group to arrive at a solution to a stated problem and a good trigger may be no more than one sentence long.

---

*Verbal Instructions:*

Take five or ten minutes to brainstorm a list of the things we need to think about when we are passing work on to colleagues. Then take a few minutes to identify the positive things we can do to ensure that when we pass information on to others, it is clear, accurate, and complete – in fact meets the 'Right First Time' standard. Start me off please with examples of the kinds of work that you pass on to other people... (if prompting is necessary, examples would be: telephone messages [informational; complaints; queries]; case notes; requests for information). Write up these answers as headings spaced generously on your flipchart.

Now, give me as many examples as you can think of of what makes the difference between passing work on effectively and passing it on badly to your internal customers. Tell me which heading (or headings) I should put each example under. (Prompting should not be necessary – it defeats the object of the exercise – but if the worst happens, the kinds of thing that 'make the difference' are:

- promptness
- correct and relevant information
- correct recipient
- clear statement of priority
- completeness – accurately passing on all information gathered up to that point
- realistic promises.)

That's generated a really comprehensive list of ways we can make a better job of passing work on to colleagues. So what stops us doing it right every time? We'll take just a few more minutes on this to think of all the steps (however small) that you can take to *improve* the way work is passed on to colleagues. Again, write up all the examples, using key words or phrases for brevity. Don't criticize or evaluate contributions. Encourage contributions for about five minutes.

---

**Figure 4.12** *Passing work to colleagues*

## Chapter Review

This chapter has focused upon the importance of achieving quality service with internal customers as a prerequisite for achieving it with external customers. The role of an internal customer working party to steer this element of the programme has been described.

The setting of learning aims derived from diagnostic research has been outlined, underpinning the design of an internal customer workshop. The training of temporary trainers and the development of trainers' notes, participants' workbooks and take-away reference materials are described, with examples of exercises, and guidance on the use of video and case studies.

# 5    Quality Action Teams

▷             SUMMARY             ◁

This chapter reviews quality action teams as part of the overall quality service training programme. Guidance is provided on the structuring of the action teams and their activities: the initial information cascade to all employees; the selection and training of team leaders, mentors and team members; the development of working materials for the teams; and the choice of pilot projects. The sequence of meetings for each team is described and the place of rewards and recognition considered.

## Introduction

Quality action teams are small groups of employees, trained in problem-solving techniques, who examine service quality issues *within their own area of work*, arrive at solutions, and (usually) implement their solutions. These quality improvements may be triggered by:

- already-identified problems;
- problems which the teams themselves diagnose;
- suggestions from line management;
- implementation of local performance standards.

However, ownership of projects is important: imposed tasks are likely to be resented by teams.

A key feature of quality action teams (QATs) is that they are composed of employees who work at a comparatively low level in the organization. The typical structure consists of a team of about five to eight members, a team leader (who may be of equal rank to members, or a junior supervisor – but definitely not a manager), and a mentor (a senior manager) who holds a watching brief over two or three quality action teams.

Essential features are that training and practical support are provided to these teams and that their achievements are recognized and rewarded by senior management, through the channel of the quality council.

The great value of QATs is that they harness the knowledge, the experience and the often-frustrated urge to improve working practices that are to be found at the 'sharp end' of service delivery. There is often a large, untapped resource of informed and constructive ideas waiting to be released.

Note, however, that some resistance may well come from managers, particularly those with an authoritarian style, who see QATs as an abdication of an asserted 'managers' right to manage', leading inexorably to full-blown workers' control and the end of civilization as we have known it. This is an issue that has to be resolved at the highest level: it ultimately boils down to a choice of management philosophies. On the one hand there is the belief that quality service can be imposed and enforced through managerial controls (but, in that case, why does the organization now need quality initiatives?). On the other, there is the belief that quality service can only be achieved through the willing efforts of the people who deliver that service. Most managers will recognize that there are quite adequate checks and balances built into the quality action programme – notably the emphasis on *local* action, the training provided for team leaders, the role of mentors as sounding boards for proposals, and the back-stop role played by the quality council.

---

PRACTICAL TIP

Resist all claims that employees low in the organizational hierarchy will not be able to contribute ideas to improve service quality.

---

## Structuring The Quality Action Programme

This subject has already been discussed in Chapter 3 as part of the overall structuring of the service quality training. To recap, the structural elements of the quality action team part of the programme are as follows:

- the steering group
- coordinators
- mentors
- team leaders
- team members.

*The steering group,* reporting to the quality council, has oversight of all quality action teams, coordinates projects that may overlap, conflict with, or duplicate others, as well as providing a forum for review of the ideas generated by QATs. The steering group is composed of representatives of team leaders, mentors and senior managers.

*A coordinator* has a liaison and trouble-shooting role between all parts of the quality action team programme; the role is likely to be undertaken by a professional trainer (in large organizations, more than one may be needed). The coordinator reports to the steering group.

*Mentors* are middle or senior managers who act as an informal sounding-board, guide and friend to two or three QATs. Their role is discussed later in this chapter. The selection and training of *team leaders* and *team members* likewise is discussed in detail in this chapter.

## Getting Started

Starting with managers, all employees need to be informed in broad outline of the QAT programme. This may be done by verbal communication through a management cascade or, if you are concerned to ensure that everyone gets the same message, with the same degree of enthusiasm, then a short booklet may be prepared and distributed to everybody (or, indeed, a combination of methods may be used). The sort of topics that the booklet or cascade should cover are listed in Figure 5.1

---

PRACTICAL TIPS

- Emphasize the benefits of quality improvements to each employee, not just to the organization a whole.
- Make it very clear that, while quality service is everyone's responsibility, membership of QATs is for enthusiastic volunteers only.

---

- What is a quality action team?
  - membership
  - what it does
  - kinds of problem it addresses

- Why does the organization need such teams?
  - market position
  - retaining customers
  - efficiency

- Who benefits from action teams?
  - team members
  - colleagues at work
  - customers

- How do teams operate?
  - voluntary
  - training provided
  - regular meetings
  - problem diagnosis and solution

- What management support will teams receive?
  - mentors
  - quality council
  - but also … team ownership of projects

- What is the timetable for implementation?
  - when will teams be up and running
  - how does the individual employee get involved

**Figure 5.1** *Topics for quality action teams' initial information booklet*

When you start to choose pilot projects it is essential to long-term success that the earliest teams that you set up are seen to be successful and careful selection is essential. There is no need to aim for an organization-wide launch (unless you are in a fairly small organization). It is better to avoid departments or sections with particularly acute problems and therefore greater risk of initial failures. It is certainly better to start with teams in areas of the organization that are keen to 'give it a try'; leave the sceptics and resisters until last and the successes of others will simply overtake them.

It is a good general principle to make membership of QATs voluntary; certainly this is a must for the pilot projects. The team members, team leaders and mentors must want their projects to succeed.

---

PRACTICAL TIPS

- Select pilot projects that stand a good chance of success.
- In the earlier stages of the programme, avoid departments or sections that offer only lukewarm support for quality initiatives.

## Selecting Team Leaders

Team leaders may be experienced non-supervisory employees or junior supervisors but should not be more senior than that. All members of teams are expected to contribute actively to problem-solving and the presence of a more senior member usually inhibits this. Team members tend to defer to seniority in discussion and also look to the senior person as the source of ideas. (A secondary benefit from the programme is that leadership of QATs provides a testing ground for potential supervisors.)

The tasks which a team leader undertakes, after training, are as follows:

- timetabling meetings and organizing facilities;
- training team members in selected problem-solving techniques, using supplied materials;
- managing group discussions;
- coping with conflict and achieving consensus within the team;
- reporting on team activities, or helping team members to make such reports.

Team leaders have to be able to encourage discussion and be receptive to new ideas. A 'can do' enthusiasm rather than a 'yes, but' negativity in their style of response is very necessary. They need to feel comfortable working with groups in the rough-and-tumble of a free-flowing debate and not be over-controlling or stifle creativity. Commitment to the idea of quality service and to the role of quality action teams is imperative.

## Selecting Mentors

As a rule, mentors will be drawn from 'upper middle' managers. They are not necessarily high-flyers, but neither are they those who are stuck in a rut with nowhere to go: they will be personally credible and well-regarded by senior management. Good organizational knowledge and political realism are useful (provided they are used to help make things happen, rather than to block initiatives). Mentors need to be supportive (without taking over control or becoming the source of 'all the answers'), approachable (but willing to stand back and let teams get on with it), constructively critical (but not perfectionists) and be committed to the quality service concept.

The role of the mentor is to:

- act as a sounding board for team proposals;
- guide teams on how their proposals may most effectively be implemented;
- help teams obtain the contacts and resources they need;
- ensure that teams are given a 'protected space' without interference from other managers.

## Selecting Team Members

Teams will consist of about five to eight members; sometimes a team may be as small as three people although this *may* be a barrier to creativity; teams larger than eight are to be discouraged. Big teams are most liable to turn into talking shops, or to divide into factions which spend their meetings playing politics rather than problem-solving.

Team members should be volunteers. They should be people who want to improve the way things are in the organization. Finding their own solutions to problems in their areas of work is one of the rewards of team membership. Another reward is the status that senior management will attach to participation in QATs. These are factors that are incompatible with compulsory membership.

In the earlier stages of team activity, it is better that teams are made up of people from the same department, though it may be useful to represent different aspects of that department's work amongst the members. The reason for this is the emphasis on *local* activity, on problem-solving within the areas of work that team members are *personally* involved in. As the process evolves and as local problems are solved, there may well remain some intractable issues that need to be tackled at an inter-departmental level. For such issues, teams with members drawn from different departments (and sometimes, too, teams with somewhat more senior members) may be appropriate. Such 'super-teams' are discussed later in this chapter.

The role of the team member is to:

- contribute first-hand knowledge of the organization;
- help to identify problems that the team could resolve;
- gather information that the team needs;
- help to develop solutions to identified problems;
- help to implement solutions.

Some team members may also represent the team when making presentations to management, seeking resources, liaising with other parties and the like.

## How Quality Action Teams Work

Each team will follow a pattern of regular, structured meetings which progress through a sequence of diagnostic activity → solution-seeking → implementing solutions, with the objective of continuous improvement in the quality of service delivered to internal and external customers. The intention is to mobilize the people who know the problems best and have most to gain from solving them. Teams may well also make recommendations on wider issues, that impinge on their work but lie outside their control, but this should be clearly seen a a secondary feature of their activities.

Within each team meeting, there will be a pattern of training of team members by the team leader, followed by use of the skills and techniques that training has just covered.

The activities of the team can be summarized as follows:

- to create an effective team for working together;
- to identify all issues that the team considers have an impact on the quality of their service to internal or external customers;
- to decide their priorities amongst the identified problems;
- to select which issues the team will handle itself;
- to select which issues the team will refer elsewhere (eg, to the quality council);
- to plan the actions the team will take to resolve the selected issues;
- to implement changes that the team has developed.

Over the project life cycle, each team will meet at least five times for training and activity; in practice, additional meetings may be needed at various stages, simply because one or other part of the process calls for extra time. Meetings may be held at any convenient regular interval; once a fortnight is often a manageable frequency. It balances the need not to lose momentum on projects against the need to carry out some data-gathering outside the meetings themselves and the need to get on with ordinary work duties in parallel with the action team.

It is probable that the first sequence of team meetings will resolve some but by no means all of the issues that the team has identified. Teams may, therefore, expect to continue through an abbreviated form of the full sequence (typically with the emphasis shifted from diagnosis to solution-finding) several times. Subsequent sequences may have meetings that are less frequent, perhaps monthly rather than fortnightly. Indeed, QATS should become a permanent part of the organizational culture – meeting far less frequently than in the initial phase, but continuing the unending quest for quality improvements.

It should be recognized that action teams call for a commitment of time from their members. Meetings at lunchtimes or after-hours may be a way of managing this, but the organization should also be prepared to support team members by adjusting their routine work-loads where necessary.

---

PRACTICAL TIP

- It is essential to provide a process for sympathetic handling of rejected ideas, to prevent loss of motivation by teams.

---

## The Sequence of Quality Action Meetings

Once teams have been selected, it is often useful to have a loosely-structured initial meeting where all members of the pilot teams can meet each other and have an informal dialogue with trainer and quality council members about the programme.

Each team will then follow a standard sequence of meetings which typically would cover the topics listed in Figure 5.2. Note the value of an interim review, at Session 3, of how effectively each team is functioning, in process terms. This review provides an opportunity for remedial action on under-performing teams. A further evaluation takes place at the end of the sequence of meetings and, possibly, at a later date (depending upon how long projects take to implement). These assessments may be linked to rewards.

*Session 1:*
- purpose of QATs
- learning to work together as a team
- assessment and rewards
- introduction to problem-solving processes
- setting objectives

*Session 2:*
- diagnostic processes
  – identifying problems: what goes wrong in relationships with internal and external customers?; what are the skill or knowledge gaps that need to be filled?; what may be system and procedural change needs?

*Session 3:*
- group problem-solving process
- examining solution options
- interim assessment of how well the team is working – a review of process, not results

*Session 4:*
- criteria for selecting solutions
- choosing priorities
- building commitment to action
- identifying barriers to making solutions work

*Session 5:*
- getting organizational acceptance of proposals
- managing rejected ideas
- identifying resources
- implementing proposals
- evaluating the results
- planning for the next sequence of meetings

**Figure 5.2** *Typical sequence of team meetings*

## Training Team Leaders

The selected (or potential) team leaders need to be trained in both the content of QAT meetings (eg, problem-solving techniques) and also the processes of facilitating such teams (eg, encouraging discussion, managing conflict). As well as factual input, they will need opportunities to practise using the materials before they get in front of a team meeting.

You should allow allow two to three days for team leader training. The training workshop should introduce the materials that team leaders will employ with their teams and give practice in running problem-solving activities within a group. The training should also consider the relationship between team leaders and mentors.

Topics to be covered include:

- presentation skills, including use of visual aids;
- effective teams (eg, using the Belbin team roles model);
- facilitation of group discussion, including:
  - listening skills
  - questioning techniques
  - how to create a safe framework for discussion (and how to respond to any difficult or hostile team members)
  - how to guide discussion, without over-controlling it (possibly including assertiveness skills);
- training team members in problem-analysing and problem-solving techniques, using pre-prepared materials;
- how to generate commitment to making changes.

The most important thing to convey to team leaders is that the effective QAT leader does not 'lead from the front'. They are not there to drive through their own point of view, but to help *all* members of the team to make a constructive contribution. Certainly, team leaders can contribute their own ideas to discussion; and when the team moves on to action planning and implementation the leader may have a more 'up front' role in making things happen. But in the earlier stages of the sequence of meetings their role is mainly about creating the right working climate, and about familiarizing the team with useful problem-solving techniques.

Another essential part of the leader role is to impart skills to the team members, using the leaders' guides prepared by the organization's trainers (or external consultants) for each of the five team meetings (see below). Leaders also need practice in handling those ideas which do not get accepted for implementation. This will require an element of tact, so that people are not discouraged from generating further ideas in the future.

## Training Mentors

Mentors require much less comprehensive training than team leaders. They are selected because they already possess the right kind of personal and managerial characteristics. They need to know  what team leaders will be doing at the various stages of the project cycle and they need to understand the kinds of skills that team leaders will need and the kinds of process issues that they may run up against.

However, their main role is one of low-key support to team leaders, helping to maintain the momentum of the quality initiative and helping to ensure that team proposals can be brought to fruition in the real world of the organization. Direct contact with the teams themselves is unusual: it would be quite exceptional for a mentor to attend a team meeting. Thus, there is more an informational training need than one of skill development and this can usually be met by means of a half- or one-day workshop. Nevertheless, this event can provide an opportunity for mentors to discuss and rehearse the kinds of problem on which they anticipate team leaders seeking their help.

## Developing Working Materials For The Teams

'Temporary trainers' such as QAT leaders need to have comprehensive, user-friendly materials prepared for them. These support materials are likely to include, as well as the initial explanatory booklet circulated to all employees, the following:

- guidance notes on how to be an effective team leader;
- sessional notes on the content of each of the five team meetings;
- visual aids – overhead projector slides or, often more conveniently, desk-top presenters;
- team members' workbooks containing exercises and notes for each meeting.

*Team leader guidance notes*
The content of these notes covers both the administrative aspects of team leadership and the skill elements. Typical contents are listed in Figures 5.3 and 5.4.

1. Administrative issues
- team size
- frequency of meetings
- finding time for meetings
- finding somewhere to meet
- preparing for each meeting
- obtaining workbooks, stationery, etc.

2. Team operational issues
- using the training materials
  - the leader's guide
  - the member's workbook
  - using desktop presenter or overhead projector
- effective and ineffective meetings
  - leadership style
  - agenda and timetable
  - control of discussion
  - getting consensus on decisions
  - building support for actions

**Figure 5.3** *Contents of guidance notes for team leaders*

- Have you got a suitable room booked?
  - is the layout of seats/tables convenient?
  - are heating and lighting satisfactory?
  - can you eliminate distractions (eg, telephones)?
  - have you organized flip-chart, OHP, etc?
- Have the time and place been confirmed to team members?
- Have team members received a note summarizing the previous meeting?
- What do you intend the meeting to achieve?
- What are the main learning points for team members?
- What problems can you anticipate?
  - with the subject matter?
  - with group process?
- What can you do about these problems?
- Have you had a dry run through the leader's materials for the next meeting?
- Have you kept your team mentor informed of what is happening?

**Figure 5.4** *Guidance notes for team leaders: meeting planner*

*Team leader's sessional notes*
These contain step-by-step notes on running each team meeting. The content will reflect the topic headings listed previously (Figure 5.2). An example of topic headings for the second session of the meetings cycle is given in Figure 5.5 and an extract from the sessional notes, covering one of these topics, is illustrated in Figure 5.6.

1. Recap on first meeting
   – the main conclusions agreed
   – the main learning points covered

2. Problem diagnostics: fact-finding
   – methods for identifying problems
   – data collection
   – filtering data
   – defining the problem

3. Closing the meeting
   – summary of the session
   – brief evaluation by team members
   – brief introduction to third meeting
   – agenda-setting for third meeting

**Figure 5.5** *Topics for second team meeting*

*During this session, we're going to look at methods for identifying problems that affect the quality of service we deliver to internal and external customers. We'll then go on to look at ways we can gather more facts about the problems we've highlighted, so that we can get a sharper definition of just what it is that needs to be changed.*
*There are several methods for diagnosing problems:*

Monitoring work performance:*there may be shortfalls against agreed standards or targets – in fact, if we do not have standards, then it is very hard to say whether or not anyone is doing their job well or badly.*

Observation: *watching and listening in the workplace will often reveal points of stress and strain where people are not performing as well as they might; it's then a matter for further investigation to find out why that is the case.*

Comparisons: *We can look at the different levels of performance achieved by different sections; or at the way that performance within a section may deteriorate over a period of time. At an individual level, we can look at high performers and low performers and ask ourselves what is it that is making the difference.*

> *We will now select one problem to use as a guinea pig for learning about problem diagnostics. Let's look for something that we are all familiar with, something that relates fairly obviously to quality of service. It needs to be a real issue and something that occurs in our part of the organization. At this stage, let's also keep the issue fairly narrowly-focused or we will be discussing it all day. What do we know about this topic?* (List responses on flip-chart.)
>
> - Allow about 10-15 minutes for this fact-generating process.
> - Encourage statements about the facts of the problem.
> - Discourage statements that dismiss the problem or claims that the reasons for the problem are 'obvious' – your aim at this stage is to get as much useful information as possible.
> - Consider whether the team needs more information about the problem and how this can be obtained
> - Make sure that all data are recorded as the session proceeds.

**Figure 5.6** *Topic extract: methods for identifying problems*

### Visual aids

Each meeting should have accompanying overhead projector slides or pre-prepared desk-top presenter sheets. The latter is more flexible since no electrical equipment is required and the material is easily portable. A desk-top presenter also offers the advantage that the back of display sheets, facing away from the audience, can contain prompting notes for the team leader.

Note the importance of large, bold typefaces which can be read across a meeting room, and the value of illustrations and the occasional cartoon for light relief.

### Team members' workbooks

These contain summary notes from the training inputs at each meeting, the written parts of group exercises and other materials used in problem-solving, plus space for each person to make their own notes on, for example, group decisions or individual action to be taken between meeting.

## Management Briefings to Action Teams

I have emphasized the importance of QATS conducting their own diagnostic activities and having ownership of improvement projects. Provided that ownership is recognized and respected, there is no reason why line managers should not also *offer* action teams some ideas on where they might most usefully direct their attention, so long as the 'offer' is one which the team can refuse. In the early life of teams it is especially important that projects are not imposed upon them and mentors may have a diplomatic role to play in some instances.

Figure 5.7 provides an outline of some issues which line managers can legitimately draw to the attention of quality action teams that are operating within their departments. The management brief should be short and as factually specific as possible about the issues raised. Opinion should be clearly distinguished from fact; any firm priorities amongst the issues should be indicated.

- Elements of corporate strategy which may be expected to impinge on the department in the future.
- Current departmental objectives and targets.
- Known performance deficiencies.
- Areas of work believed to offer the potential for performance improvements.

**Figure 5.7** *Appropriate issues for management briefs to quality action teams*

## Rewards And Recognition

The basic idea of rewards and recognition for quality service efforts was outlined in Chapter 3. Rewards include one-off cash payments and additional salary increments; 'recognition' awards have status but no pecuniary value: for example, 'employee of the month', a 'quality achievers' dinner dance and – most relevant here – the opportunity for the best proposals from quality action teams to be presented to the top management of the organization by the originating team *in person*.

It may be argued that the 'recognition' route is both more effective than the 'reward' one and usually less expensive: the associated status has longer-lasting motivational impact. An essential element of both reward and recognition schemes is publicity: principally internally, but also as useful PR targeted on external customers. All rewards and recognition should be based upon well-defined, measurable outputs that relate directly to the purposes for which the organization exists. They should not be rewards for input: if people are 'trying hard' but there is no measurable output, then the quality programme has been misconceived. Attendance at QAT meetings is not a ground for reward or recognition; it is what the team achieves that matters.

The best quantification of what QATs have achieved is to identify the specific changes that have come about in work practices as a result of the team's efforts and then to assess, as accurately as circumstances allow, the value to the organization of those changes. This is preferable to the use of subjective opinion data from internal and external customers.

Note that other, interim assessments of team effectiveness may be desirable during the meetings cycle. Such interim assessments will be concerned mainly with the processes of the team and the purpose is to ensure that corrective action can be taken in good time where a team is not addressing the right kind of issue or is experiencing serious inter-personal problems or leadership failure.

## Quality super-teams

As the locally-focused QATs progress through the meetings cycle for the second or third time, there may remain some intractable issues that need to be tackled at an inter-departmental level. For such issues, teams with members drawn from different departments may be appropriate. 'Super-teams' will follow the same pattern of operation as ordinary teams; in general they should be made up of similar type and levels of employee and there can be real value in borrowing experienced members of local teams to form the inter-departmental action groups. Sometimes it may be appropriate to form such teams so that they include more senior members, particularly if specialized technical or professional inputs are needed. However, this may still be more usefully contained by inviting senior people to attend as *ad hoc*, rather than permanent, members. For similar reasons, there occasionally may need to be quality action teams formed entirely of managers, to address high-level inter-departmental quality issues.

## Chapter Review

This chapter has reviewed the nature and activities of quality action teams and emphasized that their strength is derived from the participation of employees at the lower end of the organizational hierarchy, who are closest to the problems and often have the most direct gains from resolving them. The restricted role of management briefings to action teams has been considered.

Guidance has been provided on the structuring of the action teams and their activities, beginning with the information cascade to all employees, selection and training of team leaders, mentors and team members, the development of working materials for the teams, and leading into pilot projects. The sequence of meeting for each item has been described and the place of reward and recognition considered.

# 6  Quality Service Skills

▷ SUMMARY ◁

This chapter discusses the design of a training workshop to provide the core quality service skills. This includes the formation of a quality service skills working party, determining learning aims and the development of support materials for trainers and participants. Examples of materials are provided. The development of appropriate skills for temporary trainers is considered, with specific guidance on techniques for interpersonal skills training. Lastly, issues in the validation of quality service training are described and specimen measurement instruments illustrated.

## Introduction

This skills element in the quality service programme is the essential complement to the earlier focus upon internal customers and upon quality action teams. It deals with a group of diverse skills that have in common simply the fact that they are all concerned with the individual employee's ability to deliver quality service. These core quality service skills can be summarized as:

- getting things right first time;
- listening to customers;
- constructive complaint-handling;
- appropriately assertive behaviour under pressure;
- clear verbal and written communication;
- helpful support to colleagues.

Most of the following comments covering basic design concepts have been discussed in full detail in Chapter 4. Here, I shall simply repeat the main ideas, applied to quality service skills training.

## Designing the quality service skills training workshop.

### Diagnostic Foundations

- The training should be based upon your research into quality service problems that underpins the whole programme.
- The diagnostic data should provide convincing material for case studies and exercises.
- Identify the inter-connections between *all* the parts of the quality service programme: internal customer, performance standards, service skills, action teams, manager involvement.

### Quality Service Skills Working Party

- Form a working party, under the quality council, responsible for quality service skills training.
- Achieve a mix of expertise and authority levels.
- Set the working party to steer the design (ensuring that key issues are included), to manage the implementation (ensuring adequate resourcing), and to legitimize the process – but not to write the training material.
- Detailed preparatory work will be carried out by the training department, or by external consultants.

### Setting Learning Aims

The aims should emerge from the diagnostic data and the examples given below are just examples, not a definitive or universal list:

1. To ensure a shared understanding and common base level of competence in customer service skills by all employees.
   These skills include:

   - listening -- on the telephone and face-to-face;
   - assertiveness;
   - writing to customers, especially use of plain English;
   - effective passing on of work to colleagues/other departments;
   - handling complaints constructively;

2. To reinforce understanding of who each employee's customer is.

3. To reinforce quality improvements taking place concurrently through the standards and QATs programmes.

4. To reinforce the internal customer training.

## The Skills Workshop

Figure 6.1 provides a specimen timetable for a one-day skills workshop, based upon the aims listed above. Clearly, this can be extensively adapted according to the needs of your organization.

| Session duration | Cumulative time | Session content and objective(s) |
|---|---|---|
| 10 | 10 | Introduction to the day |
| 05 | 15 | Quiz: How customer-friendly are you? |
| 30 | 45 | Skills video episode 1 (intro.) |
|  |  | Exercise: When you were the customer... |
|  |  | Discussion: What is customer service about? |
| 25 | 1h.10 | Skills video episode 2 (complaint overview) plus review sheet and discussion (complaints as opportunities ) |
| 20 | 1h.30 | Tea/coffee break |
| 10 | 1h.40 | Corporate standards and customer service |
| 40 | 2h.20 | Skills video episode 3 (listening), plus review sheet and group discussion |
|  |  | Small group exercise on listening skills |
| 60 | 3h.20 | Skills video episode 4 (assertiveness), plus review sheet |
|  |  | Group discussion |
|  |  | Small group exercise on assertiveness |
| 55 | 4h.15 | Lunch |
| 40 | 4h.55 | Corporate standards style guide, group discussion |
|  |  | Small group exercise: Use of clear English |
| 30 | 5h.25 | Skills video episode 5 (passing work to colleagues... helpfully), plus review sheet |
|  |  | Group discussion |
|  |  | Brainstorming exercise |
| 15 | 5h.40 | Tea/coffee break |
| 30 | 6h.10 | Personal action planning and group feedback |
| 15 | 6h.25 | Customer service skills: a summary, plus questions |
| 20 | 6h.45 | Assessment session |
| 05 | 6h.50 | Skills video episode 6 (recap) |
|  |  | Close of workshop |

**Figure 6.1** *Specimen timetable: one-day quality service skills workshop*

## Support Materials for the Training Programme

These are likely to include the following:

- managers' briefing note for use in information cascade;
- notes and visual aids for use by the temporary trainers running skills workshops;
- training of trainers workshop to prepare the temporary trainers, especially for the interpersonal skills elements of the programme;
- participants' workbook (exercises and handout notes used during the event);
- video material integrated with the workshop objectives and other content (purpose-made, or hired).

The *managers' briefing note* will be a short description of the purposes and content of the skills training, it may usefully emphasise the value of managers' reinforcement of newly-trained skills back in the workplace.

The *trainers' notes* and accompanying visual aids (overhead slides or desk-top presenter format) need to be clear and comprehensive, especially if they are to be used by the pool of temporary trainers. There must be clear cross-references to group exercises and to any reference notes for participants. The use of video (if any) must be integrated with the material and overhead slides or presenter sheets clearly linked to the text.

It is helpful – especially to temporary trainers – for each of the sessional notes to follow a standard format. This helps to achieve a consistent quality in the training as well as providing a check that no important element of the training design has been missed. The standardized format suggested in Chapter 4 is reproduced in Figure 6.2 for your convenience.

---

- Introductory comments by the trainer, bridging from the previous activity.
- Statement of the formal learning objective(s) that relate to that session.
- Presentation to the audience (factual information, description and illustration of skills, and so on), comprising:
  - key points summary of training inputs;
  - lead-in remarks for activities ('Why we're doing this exercise'; 'What steps you should follow').
- Activities by trainees connecting learning points to trainees' own work experience (questions, discussion, practice of skills, paper-based exercises, and so on).
- Key points debriefing of the session (trigger questions to use; making the transfer to work; summary review of learning points).
- Lead-in remarks for the next session.

---

**Figure 6.2** *Standard format for session design*

In similar fashion, a standard format can be adopted for each practical exercise; see Figure 6.3.

- Explanation of 'Why we're doing this exercise'.
- Description of the steps the participants should follow, including any division of trainees into sub-groups and the introduction of any support materials (such as behaviour observation checklists).
- Running the exercise (including any interim reviews, correction of errors, etc. as appropriate).
- Whole group ('plenary') debriefing of the exercise, including use of trigger questions to provoke debate, reinforce learning and encourage transfer of new knowledge and skills into the trainees' work.

**Figure 6.3** *Standard format for group exercises*

Even temporary trainers should not be perceived to be reading from a script. However, it is very important where trainers personalize the material that key points are not watered down and that the trainer conveys a clear commitment to the purposes of the workshop.

Figures 6.4 to 6.6 show an example of notes for temporary trainers on an opening session of a quality service skills workshop:

- Figure 6.4 comprises guidance notes for the trainer;
- Figure 6.5 is a trainer's copy of the quiz for participants;
- Figure 6.6 offers the trainer a set of answers to the quiz.

*Duration:* 5 minutes

*Commentary:* This is a very short 'ice-breaker' activity to get the group talking.

*Formal objectives:*
- Participants will recognize examples of the customer service issues that the workshop will be tackling.
- Group members will actively participate in the training.

*Trainer Input:*
- This is a short warm-up exercise to start us off thinking about customer service issues. (*Issue copies of the quiz.*)
- We'll go through it quickly, question by question. Who is going to start me off on question 1? (*Note that 'answer sheet' follows.*)
- Let's move on now with a short piece of film, showing some typical person-in-the-street comments about customer service expectations. Afterwards, we'll also look at your own personal experiences of being customers – and what we can learn from that.

**Figure 6.4** *Trainer's sessional notes: 'How customer-friendly are you?'*

*Quiz: 'How customer-friendly are you?'*

1. If customers do not complain, does that mean that our organization is doing a great job?

2. We have thousands of customers: does it matter if we lose one dissatisfied customer?

3. Do customers whose complaint has been dealt with stay with us?

4. What are the advantages of making it difficult for complainants to get through on the telephone?

5. Who are my customers?

6. Are there officially laid down standards that describe the quality of service we should be providing?

**Figure 6.5** *Trainer's sessional notes: 'How customer-friendly are you?' – quiz for participants*

Note that there is no requirement for participants' answers to match word-for-word your answer sheet. What matters is that their answers echo the spirit of the correct response.

Q1. No – only a minority of people ever complain to the organization; many more people simply stop doing business with us; and most of those who do not complain to us directly, still complain to all their friends and acquaintances.

Q2. Yes – there is evidence that one dissatisfied customer may spread their bad feelings to scores of other people – all representing a potential loss of customer support over many years.

Q3. Customers who have had a complaint dealt with efficiently and courteously often become the most loyal customers of all, because they appreciate the care and personal service that they have received.

Q4. None. Even if you gain a temporary escape from complaints, the customer will eventually make their complaint known – and they are then more likely to be very 'steamed up' about it.

Q5. The answer should reflect both external customers and internal customers (supply locally-appropriate examples)

Q6. Yes – corporate and local standards set measurable requirements for service quality.

**Figure 6.6** *Trainer's sessional notes: 'How customer-friendly are you?' – trainer's answers to quiz*

## Training of Trainers Workshop

All trainers – full-time or temporary – need to familiarize themselves with new material. Temporary trainers are likely also to need to develop their ability to deliver interpersonal skills training. It is more economical to carry out a limited form of trainer-training wholly within the framework of practising to deliver the quality skills training event, rather than go through a full-blown process of trainer-training. Topics such as presentation, running exercises, giving feedback to trainees and the like can be covered using the materials which the temporary trainers will subsequently deliver.

The trainer skills which temporary trainers may find most difficult are those relating to group process and interpersonal skills. In Chapter 4 guidance was offered on the effective use of video material. What follow are guidance notes on:

- group discussion;
- interpersonal skills training;
- using role play;
- encouraging transfer of learning.

### Guidance notes on group discussion

1. Encourage group members to answer their colleagues' queries; similarly, when questions have been incorrectly answered, look to group members to correct or expand on the answer. Only supply the answers yourself if no one volunteers, or if several people have got the answer wrong.

2. Encourage the flow of discussion within the group as much as between individual members and yourself. This increases group participation and learning (people often learn better from their colleagues than from the person in the training role) and saves you from the trap of being seen as the only source of information.

3. When you need comments from everyone in the group, ask for these in a random order, jumping around the group. Going round in the order in which people are sitting (the 'creeping death' approach) often provokes anxiety in those at the end of the line. A random approach also keeps everyone alert since each may be next.

4. Group discussion is not (primarily) provided as an opportunity for theoretical discussions of the training topic. Use group discussion to trigger consideration of the implications for the way that participants do their own jobs.

5. Avoid fight-to-the-death debate with someone who disagrees with you:

- attack the ideas, not the person;
- remain good humoured;
- broaden the debate so that other group members can respond to that individual.

*Guidance notes on interpersonal skills training*

1. Ensure that you have clear, specific learning objectives. Dump pseudo-objectives that talk about 'good attitude'. For a full discussion of writing behavioural objectives, the reader is recommended to consult the works of Robert Mager.[1]

2. An invaluable tool for interpersonal skills training is the 'behaviour observation checklist'. Behaviour observation data show whether or not people can perform the skills which the training has tried to impart. Such checklists can be used by observers during role plays and by managers to reinforce or assess workplace behaviours. An example is provided in Figure 6.7.

3. An effective behaviour observation checklist has the following features:

- each item of behaviour relates to a training objective;
- each item is observable – not something to be inferred;
- the layout makes the checklist easy to use; plus, sometimes,
- each item is illustrated by positive and negative examples.

4. An intrinsic part of interpersonal skills training, though one which some people find discomforting, is that of giving the individual feedback on his or her performance in the skill. Feedback should help the learner, not serve as an excuse for the trainer to let off steam; reinforcement of good practices through praise is even more important than correction of errors.

5. Feedback should be brief – make only the most important points – and be given as soon as possible after the observed behaviour has occurred. Comments need to be specific, rooted in the detail of observed behaviour, communicated in plain English, and must make judgements solely against criteria that had previously been set for the activity.

6. Resistance to feedback is usually a sign that the comments are accurate but uncomfortable; however, resistance is sometimes justified because the comments reflect poor observation. The trainer should not react to resistance as if it were a personal attack and should try to get the trainee to talk about the feelings of resistance themselves, rather than the subject matter of the exercise.

| TELEPHONE USER TRAINING | Observer: | Trainee: | Date: |
|---|---|---|---|
| **Behaviour categories** | **Examples of relevant behaviour (circle instances observed)** | | |
| | **POSITIVE EXAMPLES** | **NEGATIVE EXAMPLES** | |
| Greets caller | Uses caller's surname. Identifies self. Uses good morning (etc.) | Omits caller's/own name. Uses caller's first name. | |
| Establishes the purpose of the call | Asks open and probing questions. Gives verbal summary of purpose. | No clear purpose. Waffles. Fails to gather information needed. No summary. | |
| Chooses appropriate language | No jargon, company abbreviations, or technical terms. Does not talk down. | Confusing use of jargon, etc. Use of emotive words. Patronizing tone. | |
| Uses courteous tone of voice | Clear. Interesting tone. Varies pace. Conveys warmth. | Mumbles. Monotonous tone. Speaks too fast. Sounds coldly bureaucratic. Aggressive. | |
| Handles complaints constructively | Listens carefully. Gives summary. Involves customer in solution. Proposes actions. | Becomes defensive/ aggressive. Argues the facts. No solution proposed. | |
| Provides information that customer needs | Checks need. Give information clearly. Is accurate. Clarifies if necessary. | Misunderstands need. Inaccurate. Unclear. Ignores/ mishandles questions. | |
| Closes call well | Thanks caller. Summarizes conversation. | Abrupt close. No summary of action. | |

**Figure 6.7** *Example of behaviour observation checklist*

***Guidance notes on using role play***

1. Role play allows safe practice of interpersonal skills in the workplace. It may usefully be combined with video and enables people to practise skills that the video has demonstrated.

2. Much of the value of role play comes from structured feedback to the role player. Such feedback should be concerned with how well the appropriate behaviours have been used, not with the person's acting ability. It is often helpful to undertake role plays in threesomes – two people being the main parties in the fictitious action and the third being the observer.

3. The value of the observer's feedback is enhanced if he or she uses a behaviour observation checklist during the role play. This ensures that the correct behaviours are reinforced, rather than the observer's subjective judgements of what those ought to be.

4. It is the role player's real feelings and behaviour that matter. Playing at being someone else simply distances the experience and reduces the scope for learning to take place.

*Guidance notes on encouraging transfer of learning*

1. Do not take it for granted that what someone appears to have learned on a course will be put into practice.

2. Brief people before training so that they know what pay-offs their manager expects them to get from the training.

3. Make action planning an ongoing process, not something crammed into the final hour of a course, when people are thinking about their journeys home. Doing it session-by-session ensures that important points do not get forgotten.

4. Design learning sessions so that each element is linked to a question about 'How does this apply to my job?' Figure 6.8 provides an example of a checklist to review the applications from a training event.

5. Arrange that managers de-brief returning trainees to check out what they have learned. Action planning notes or checklists used within the training can provide a ready-made framework for such discussions. Agree a timetable for putting these skills or knowledge into practice.

---

1. From this learning event (or, session), what do I most want to:
   - put to use as soon as possible?
   - get more diagnostic information about?
   - get external help for?
2. How do my action points connect with corporate purposes?
3. What training might I need?
4. What management actions may be needed?
5. What procedural changes may be needed?
6. Who will do what, when?

---

**Figure 6.8** *Checklist for transfer of learning*

## Participants' Materials

The practical exercises and reference notes can be comb-bound or similarly presented. This increases the likelihood that the material will be retained by the participants. An example of the integration of the trainers' notes and the participants' wordbook is given in Figures 6.9 to 6.12, for a session on 'listening to customers':

- Figure 6.9 comprises the trainer's sessional notes;
- Figure 6.10 a video review sheet;
- Figure 6.11 a summary handout for participants;
- Figure 6.12 provides a checklist for the observer during a role play exercise.

*Duration*: 40 minutes

*Learning objective:* Trainees will demonstrate competence in listening to customers, on the telephone and face-to-face.

*Trainer input: (Issue the video review sheet)*

1. Instruct the group:
   - to glance through the questions
   - to watch the video without distractions
   - to complete the review sheet afterwards.

Show the 'listening' episode of the skills video; then switch off the monitor again.

2. Start the group discussion with quick responses to the review sheet questions. Conclude by running through the 'key points' on effective listening and then issue the summary handout.

3. Introduce the exercise, 'Hearing what you don't want to hear': the purpose of the exercise is to improve your listening skills by providing you with an opportunity to listen to views with which you normally disagree. You will work in trios for this exercise. In each trio you will each in turn be speaker, listener, and observer. Decide the order in which you will each take on these roles.

Each of you should pick a subject about which you hold fairly strong opinions, but not a technically-specialized issue requiring expert knowledge. It should be a matter of general knowledge or current affairs to which some degree of controversy attaches. The subject that you choose will be the one that you have to listen to.

The person who will be talking to you, while you listen, will talk for four or five minutes (at most) to present the case *against* your preferred viewpoint. As listener, your task is to listen effectively in the way that this skill has been presented in the workshop. The speaker should put more emphasis on the facts of the case than on appeals to emotion. The speaker's objective is to make effective listening a challenging but achievable task for the listener.

The observer's task is to use the checklist (Figure 6.12) to note examples of good and bad listening on the part of the listener. The observer does not need to assess the performance of the speaker at all. At the end, the observer should give feedback to the listener on how effectively he or she has used the skills of good listening. It's very important that observers base their feedback only on what they actually hear happening in front of them.

(*Allow five minutes for each listener, plus about ten minutes total for the feedback by observers. Take just a few minutes at the end for general feedback from the trios about what kinds of difficulty they might have experienced in listening effectively. Repeat the point that listening is a skill that improves with practice and if you don't listen you'll never know if you are tackling the* right *quality service problem.*)

4. Moving on, one of the problems we sometimes have to cope with when listening to customers is the person who is very angry or even abusive. So in the next session, we'll look at what we can do in such circumstances to politely but firmly assert ourselves.

**Figure 6.9** *Trainer's sessional notes: listening to customers*

- List the two main reasons why Mr Brown is angry
- List three good things that Sue Green does to take the heat out of the situation
- List three good things that Sue does to resolve Mr Brown's problems
- List as many things as you can think of that are done badly by the angry clerk in the final scene.

**Figure 6.10** *Trainer's sessional notes: listening to customers. Video review sheet: episode on listening skills*

1. Effective listening means: *they* talk, *you* listen (80:20 or even 90:10)
   - let them get it off their chest
   - don't interrupt (unless they're way off the subject)
   - listen; don't be busy planning your answer
   - make notes of key points
2. Check out that you have understood what has been said:
   - ask questions to clarify anything you are unsure about
   - give 'reflective summaries'
   - don't 'tune out' the things that you might be less pleased to hear
3. Demonstrate you are listening by:
   - eye contact
   - body posture
   - interested tone of voice
4. Treat listening to customers as the diagnostic first step in finding a workable solution to their problem:

- don't argue, defend, or excuse
- admit mistakes and apologize
- always offer to help – never, 'It's not my job'
- get the facts; don't jump to conclusions
- look for positive actions *you* can take

5. Build the relationship with the customer:
   - show that you can see things from their point of view
   - use the other person's name
   - focus upon positive action for the future, rather than raking over history
   - include them as contributors to your planned actions – 'We can sort this out together…'.

**Figure 6.11** *Trainer's sessional notes: listening to customers. Handout for participants: effective listening*

|  | YES | NO |
|---|---|---|
| Listens, not talks: | | |
| – ratio of speaker to listener about 80:20 | | |
| – if speaker is angry, lets him/her let off steam | | |
| – does not interrupt | | |
| – brings straying speaker back onto subject | | |
| – makes notes of key points | | |
| Checks out understanding of what has been said: | | |
| – asks clarifying questions | | |
| – gives 'reflective summaries' | | |
| – accurately hears 'uncomfortable' facts | | |
| Demonstrates listening: | | |
| – eye contact | | |
| – body posture | | |
| – interested tone of voice | | |
| Listens as means of finding a workable solution: | | |
| – doesn't argue, defend, or excuse | | |
| – admits mistakes and apologizes | | |
| – doesn't blame others | | |
| – offers to help | | |
| – gets the facts | | |
| – doesn't jump to conclusions | | |
| – looks for positive actions he/she can take | | |
| Builds the relationship with the customer: | | |
| – puts herself/himself on speaker's side | | |
| – actively looks for ways to solve the problem | | |

**Figure 6.12** *Trainer's sessional notes: listening to customers. Hearing what you don't want to hear – observer's checklist*

## Production of Video Material

Chapter 4 contains notes on the effective use of video in training. Here I shall outline the content of a trigger video designed to help people to learn about the skills involved in quality service.

The film should consist of several short episodes, of two to four minutes' duration, totalling about 20 minutes in all. Separate the episodes by about 20 seconds of plain-coloured blank screen to give the trainer time for switching equipment on and off; a ten-second countdown clock on screen can be helpful in cueing each episode.

The content of the film should illustrate behaviour relating to quality service skills, using situations, locations and actors that reflect conditions and personnel in the organization using the material. Trainees are notorious for playing the game of 'we're not like that' in order to discount training messages, however intrinsically valid, where those messages are conveyed in situations that do not match their own experience of the organization.

By and large, you get what you pay for when it comes to commissioning video material. Whatever the investment, however, you need to ensure that you *are* getting what you want. Some video production houses adopt an extraordinarily arrogant attitude towards clients, taking the position that once an initial brief has been agreed, the creative implementation is entirely in their hands until the finished product emerges.

On the contrary, the client must be involved at all stages from initial scripting, selection of acting personnel, choice of sets and external locations, through to shooting and editing. It is, of course, a recipe for disaster if there are two people, the client and the video company's director, both trying to direct the production. But it is often very important for the client to be on location for the shoot so that any fine-tuning of the script and the presentation can be made on the basis of real knowledge of the organization.

The content of the episodes in the quality skills video will be determined by the workshop objectives and by the appropriateness of the video medium. For example, the skill area concerned with clear written communications is better handled using paper-based materials than video. The quality service skills topics, listed earlier are:

1. getting things right first time;
2. listening to customers;
3. constructive complaint-handling;
4. appropriately assertive behaviour under pressure;
5. clear verbal and written communication;
6. helpful support to colleagues.

Of these, number 1 and the part of number 5 relating to written communication are not readily illustrated by video, whereas interpersonal skills such as numbers 2, 3, 4 and 6 can be demonstrated on screen. To these training topics you may wish to add an introduction, such as brief 'vox pop' comments about quality service by customers (real ones or actors) and a concluding recap that shows a key moment from each of the main episodes.

Incidentally, it is generally desirable to avoid the 'bad example – good example' formula. The repetition of each episode in two versions greatly increases the time spent in passive viewing (and the production costs); also, bad instances are often more memorable than the good. It is preferable to make each self-contained episode mostly good or mostly bad. The good examples are used to illustrate 'how to do it'; the bad examples provide a trigger for group discussion of how trainees feel about that sort of situation and the behaviour illustrated, and what they would do differently.

One final point: effective video does not stand alone. Ensure that the video is created concurrently with and complementary to all other components of the training event. A film must be an integrated part of the learning process, not a bit of light entertainment tacked on to fill in the after-lunch spot.

## Validation of Quality Service Training

Any trainer with a concern for the cost-effectiveness of training will want to know whether that training is achieving what it was meant to do. A full consideration of validation is outside the scope of this book (for detailed guidance, see *Validating Your Training*[2]). However, it is possible to show some examples of the application of validation techniques to quality service training.

First, though, it is important to clarify why the traditional end-of-course 'happy sheet' is not an adequate method of validation. The major limitations of the happy sheet are that:

- it does not measure actual learning – and trainees' self-perceptions of their learning are often very unreliable;
- it cannot predict whether learning will transfer into the workplace – what trainees say and what actually happens may diverge widely;
- it does not reliably assess the effectiveness of the training methods, nor that of the trainers themselves; such judgements are far too easily swayed by personal feelings that bear no relationship to the amount of learning achieved.

Happy sheets are not improved by being subjected to statistical analysis, nor by dressing them up in computerized formats. There is no value in a detailed statistical analysis of data that is itself unreliable and the phrase 'garbage in, garbage out' might well have been invented for end-of-course reviews!

Any test of learning is valid only so long as it accurately reflects the objectives of that learning. There are different kinds of learning that people experience as part of training activities. Some kinds of learning are mainly cognitive ('intellectual') in nature – for example, knowing what different departments do, or correctly knowing a procedural sequence. Other kinds of learning involve what are called psycho-motor skills. These involve skills of co-ordinating body and mind. Riding a bicycle, driving a car, typing at a keyboard are all examples. A third category consists of interpersonal skills: behaviour between people – verbal (your choice of words, tone of voice, listening accuracy) and physical (body posture and gestures).

Different kinds of learning need to be assessed by different test methods. In summary, these associations are as follows:

- cognitive learning – written (or verbal) test using a question and answer approach;
- psycho-motor skills – practical test requiring demonstration of skills in realistic situations;
- interpersonal skills – structured behaviour observation in as realistic a situation as can be contrived.

The ability to state (whether verbally or in writing) the correct answer to a question about a skill represents only a cognitive test – the person may know the right answer *in theory*. It does not measure that person's ability to *use* the skills in real situations. It is preferable to test what people have learned from a training course (or other learning activity) subsequent to that event, and to test it in the workplace. An example of a validation instrument using behaviour observation to assess training concerned with handling customer complaints is given in Figure 6.13; Figures 6.14 and 6.15 provide an example using a written test to assess the same training topic of complaint-handling. A comparison of the two approaches should give you an idea of the strengths and limits of each, in relation to skills training and to cognitive material.

*Instructions to the Supervisor*

1. Try to complete the form about three weeks after completion of training.
2. Only record what you actually see or hear at first hand.
3. Tick each example of positive or negative behaviour.
4. Put a total for the positive and negative ticks in the sub-total columns for each topic area.

*Name of person being assessed* . . . . . . . . . . . . . . . . . . . . . . . .

*Date(s) when assessment completed*. . . . . . . . . . . . . . . . . . .

*Name of supervisor conducting assessment* . . . . . . . . . . . . . . . . . .

| Behaviours to be assessed | Evidence for the assessed behaviours<br>POSITIVE EXAMPLES | YES | NO | NEGATIVE EXAMPLES | YES | NO |
|---|---|---|---|---|---|---|
| Complaint-handling | Leaves caller pleased<br>Receives compliments on handling problem<br>Offers to help – 'Let's see what we can do to sort this out'<br>Caller states expectations not met<br>Emphasizes what he/she can do for customer<br>Focus on corrective action, not raking over history<br>Does not retaliate/argue/become defensive<br>Keeps a calm tone of voice<br>Admits mistakes and apologizes<br>Only promises what he/she can deliver<br>Explores options where appropriate<br>Does not jump to conclusions<br>Lets angry customers blow off steam before moving on to get at the details | | | Makes it difficult for complainants to get through<br>Blames other departments or the computer<br>Hides behind unexplained statements about 'company policy'<br>Emphasizes what he/she can't do for customer<br>Hides in jargon<br>Delays in responding to enquiry/complaint<br>Unprofessional behaviour: indifference, rudeness<br>'It's not my job/department'<br>Leaves caller annoyed; frustrated | | |
| *Sub-totals for complaint-handling* | | | | | | |

**Figure 6.13** *Quality service skills: complaint-handling. Supervisor's assessment sheet*

1. State two positive benefits that can be obtained from customers' complaints.

2. List four common causes of customer complaints.

3. When you are responding to a complaint, what are four positive things that should underlie the tone and general direction of your response to the customer?

4. When you move on to deal with the substance of the complaint, what are four of the steps you should take?

5. In handling a complaint, list four kinds of verbal behaviour that you should avoid.

**Figure 6.14** *Quality service skills: complaints-handling. Written test*

*All marks out of 4.*

Q1. State two positive benefits that can be obtained from customers' complaints.
*Award 2 points for each correct answer, up to 4 points maximum.*

- opportunity to improve the organization's work practices
- opportunity to create a customer who is actually more satisfied than one who has not needed to complain
- opportunity for you to work in a more professional manner

Q2. List four common causes of customer complaints.
*Award 1 point for each correct answer, up to 4 maximum.*

- unmet expectations in quality of products or service
- limited choices within product and service ranges
- frustration from errors *or* from unclear communications
- delays in deliveries or response to enquiries
- unprofessional behaviour (eg, indifference, rudeness)
- difficulties getting in touch with the organization

Q3. When you are responding to a complaint, what are four positive things that should underlie the tone and general direction of your response to the customer?
*Award 1 point for each correct answer, up to 4 maximum.*

- keep a calm tone of voice
- always offer to help – never 'It's not my job/my department'
- emphasize what you can do for them, not what you can't do
- focus on corrective action, not raking over history
- get onto adult-to-adult level – 'tell me the facts'
- put yourself on their side.

Q4. When you move on to deal with the substance of the complaint, what are four of the steps you should take?
*Award 1 point for each correct answer, up to 4 maximum.*

- agree that the problem exists
- explore options where appropriate
- say what you'll do (with realistic promises)
- restate your understanding of the situation as a check and to show you have listened
- show respect for the customer's situation
- show empathy – putting yourself in their shoes
- admit mistakes and apologize
- identify who you are

Q5. In handling a complaint, list four kinds of verbal behaviour that you should avoid.
*Award 1 point for each correct answer, up to 4 maximum.*

- retaliation
- argument
- becoming defensive
- jumping to conclusions
- blaming other departments, the computer, or yourself
- hiding in jargon, or unexplained statements about 'company policy'

**Figure 6.15** *Quality service skills: complaints-handling. Assessors' marking scheme for written test*

## Chapter review

This chapter has provided guidance on how to design and deliver a short workshop on quality service skills. It must be emphasized that this skills training is only one of the range of measures that must be integrated in a comprehensive quality programme in order to change the entrenched practices of any organization.

Pursuing 'quality' in all aspects of service delivery may seem daunting or perhaps even unnecessary. But no organization – in commercial, public or voluntary sectors – can take it for granted that the people whose needs it exists to serve will continue to come back, regardless of how they are treated. Expectations of quality service are continually rising: the choice is to soar with the eagles, or to squabble amongst the turkeys. Which kind of organization would you prefer to work in?

NOTES
1. For example, R Mager, *Preparing Instructional Objectives* (2nd edn), 1991, Kogan Page.
2. Tony Newby, *Validating Your Training*, 1992, Kogan Page

# Index